James Erskine Calder

Some account of the Wars, Extirpation, Habits, etc.

Of the Native Tribes of Tasmania

James Erskine Calder

Some account of the Wars, Extirpation, Habits, etc.
Of the Native Tribes of Tasmania

ISBN/EAN: 9783337267964

Printed in Europe, USA, Canada, Australia, Japan

Cover: Foto ©ninafisch / pixelio.de

More available books at **www.hansebooks.com**

SOME ACCOUNT

OF THE

WARS, EXTIRPATION, HABITS, &c.,

OF THE

NATIVE TRIBES

OF

TASMANIA:

BY J. E. CALDER.

Tasmania :
HENN AND CO., PRINTERS, 12 & 75 ELIZABETH STREET,
HOBART TOWN.

1875.

TO GEORGE WHITCOMB, ESQUIRE,

THE INTIMATE FRIEND OF TASMANIA'S GREATEST BENEFACTOR

GEORGE AUGUSTUS ROBINSON,

This volume, embodying an account of his services and exploits, is inscribed by

J. E. CALDER.

June, 1876.

I have said elsewhere that in preparing the foregoing narrative I have had the great advantage of consulting the immense correspondence on the subject of the aborigines of Tasmania which is deposited in the office of the Colonial Secretary; and take this opportunity to express my acknowledgements to such of the gentlemen of that department who kindly facilitated the tedious work of reference thereto, namely the chief of the office staff B. T. SOLLY ESQUIRE, and his assistants Messieurs H. F. SMITH and R. NEWMAN.

J. E. C.

NOTE.—This account of the Aboriginal Inhabitants of Tasmania, is compounded of three papers written by me,—one published in the *Australasian* in 1872, a second in the *Mercury*, 1874, and the other in the *Tasmanian Tribune*, 1875.

J. E. CALDER,
August, 1875.

SOME ACCOUNT

OF THE
WARS, EXTIRPATION, HABITS, &c.,

OF THE
NATIVE TRIBES OF TASMANIA.

By J. E. Calder.

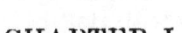

CHAPTER I.

The most interesting event in the history of Tasmania, after its discovery, seems to me to be the extinction of its ancient inhabitants; and as the causes that have led thereto have been only imperfectly told, I purpose throwing a little more light on the subject than has, as yet, been made public, which I derive from authentic official documents—not generally perused by writers on the colonies—that I have had the rare advantage of studying, and which contain, also, copious accounts of their wars on the whites, and some information about their habits.

It is believed they were never a numerous people, and at no period since the colonisation of the country, in 1803, do they seem to have exceeded 7,000—which may be safely taken as an outside estimate of their numbers.

One individual of the race is now its only living representative, a very old woman, known amongst the colonists by the name of Lalla, but whose native name is Truganini.

The first settlers after landing on these shores, lived peaceably in their new possession for several months before the two races came to blows; and the hostility thus begun continued, with no great intermission, until, and only ended with, the removal of the last of the blacks to Wyba Luma, which was the name they gave to their asylum on Flinders Island.

The first landing of the white pioneers of the colony took place on the 13th of June, 1803 (Evans, Bent.). The party located themselves on the shores of a little bay, which they called Risdon, about three or four miles north-easterly of Hobart Town, and on the opposite side of the Derwent. It consisted of a few soldiers, civil officers, and convicts, all under the command of Capt. Bowen, of the Royal Navy. They hutted themselves at Risdon, and remained in undisturbed possession of their encampment till the 3rd of May, 1804, when it was that the first *rencontre* took place between the soldiers and the blacks.

A few months before this last-named date, the first Governor of Tasmania (Colonel Collins) arrived here from Port Phillip, and fixed himself at Hobart Town, but without removing Bowen's little party from Risdon, which remained there under the independent command of that officer, who was superseded by the Governor five days after the skirmish, but not in consequence of it, as he had nothing to do with it.

At 11 o'clock of the morning of the 3rd of May the shouts of the natives were heard on the Risdon hills, as they drove a herd of kangaroos before them. They were armed with waddies only (short thick hunting clubs), and were accompanied by their women and children—a certain proof that they had no hostile intentions against anyone at the time, as it was their constant rule to leave them behind when they went out to fight. An eye-witness of the events of this deplorable day, of the name of White, who gave evidence on the 16th March, 1830, to a number of gentlemen, styled the Aboriginal Committee, thus describes the approach of the natives. He says ;—"I was hoeing new ground near the creek. Saw 300 of the natives come down in a circular form, and a flock of kangaroos hemmed in between them. There were men, women, and children. They looked at me with all their eyes. I went down to the creek and reported them to some soldiers." It would seem that these savages were at this time unacquainted of the occupation of their country by Europeans, this witness saying, "Is sure they did not know there was a white man in the country when they came down to Risdon." A quarrel soon took place but it is not quite certain who began it ; though, in balancing the evidence, the blacks seem to have been the aggressors. Captain Bowen was just then absent, on a visit to Slopen Island, and the troops were, at the moment, under the command of Lieutenant Moore.

The testimony of several witnesses was taken by the committee touching this unhappy event, which was generally confirmatory of White's, except that he—who was the only one actually present at the moment—declared, in opposition to all the rest, that the soldiers began the fight that took place, and *not* the blacks.

The following extract from the committee's report of the 19th March, 1830, thus sums up the evidence they took on this head :— " The committee have some difficulty in deciding whether it is to be considered as originating in an aggression by the natives, calling forth measures of self-defence, or in an attack upon them commenced by the settlers and military, under an impression that an attempt was about to be made on their position, by the unusually augmented numbers of the natives. It appears unquestionable that a person named Burke, whose habitation was considerably advanced beyond the rest, was driven from it by the natives, whose number was estimated at upwards of 500 (that is, by some of the witnesses), and much violence was threatened by them towards this man, his wife, and dwelling. . . . But whatever may have been the actual course of previous events, it is indisputable that a most lamentable encounter did at this time take place, in which the numbers of slain, men, women, and children have been estimated as high as 50; although the committee, from the experience they have had in the course of this enquiry of the facility with which numbers are magnified, as well as from other statements contradictory of the above, are induced to hope that the estimate is greatly overrated." One of the witnesses, the Rev. Mr. Knopwood, who was in the colony at the time, said he "does not know how many natives were killed, but supposes five or six."

Another battle is said to have been fought some time after on the ground where the Hobart Town Hospital now stands, in which artillery is supposed to have been used against the blacks. But this oft-told tale seems to rest on no better proof than that a little grape-shot was afterwards found, and some skeletons disinterred, at this place. Mr. Knopwood disposes of this fable in his evidence thus :—" There were no natives killed upon the hospital hill at Hobart Town. Some shot and skeletons were found there some years after the settlement was formed—the shot were the remains of stores brought from Port Phillip, and the bones those of persons who arrived from India, died, and were buried there."

Numerous fictitious fights are recorded as having taken place in the early times of the colony, and which, though still repeated by lovers of the marvellous and horrible, were found to be utterly false on investigation. Thus, some time in 1828, a party of military and police, who were sent in pursuit of the blacks, instead of acting against them, lay idly by in the bush, and on returning to their station reported a success over the enemy, having killed seven of them, they said; which rumour soon magnified into, first, 17, then 40, 50, 70, and finally 100 (as stated in Mr. Gilbert Robertson's evidence, 3rd March, 1830). They surprised them, they said, in a ravine, a perfect *cul de sac*, from which there was no escaping. Another gentleman, also a Mr. Robertson—who, like his namesake, discredited the story, proceeded next day to the field of slaughter, along with one of the heroes of the fight, a corporal of the 40th Regiment; but, on reaching the ravine, the only victims of their fury were found to be three dead dogs. The soldier then said—"To tell you the truth, we did not kill any of them; we had been out a long time, and had done nothing, and said it in bravado."—(Evidence, 4th March, 1830.) These two examples of a hundred such battles will probably be enough.

That many hostile collisions occurred between the two races during the 30 years that succeeded the first colonisation of the country is true enough; but I know of no trustworthy record of more than one, two, three, or at most four persons being killed in any one encounter. The warfare, though pretty continuous, was rather a petty affair, with grossly exaggerated details—something like the story of the hundred dead men, reduced, on inquiry, to three dead dogs.

The gradual decrease and final extinction of the ancient inhabitants of Tasmania, which is now so very nearly accomplished, is assignable to very different causes than the hostility of the whites, to which it has been so much the fashion to ascribe it; for, up to the time of their voluntary surrender to the local Government, they not only maintained their ground everywhere (the towns excepted), but had by far the best of the fight. Tribal dissensions, causing mutual destruction (for such were their jealousies and hatreds, that they fought one another all the time they were thrashing the whites), contributed to their decrease in some degree, and the justly provoked hostility of the settlers aided the progress of their decay, but only in minor manner; for, beyond all doubt, they were no match for the blacks in bush fighting, either in defensive or offensive operations. The settler and his homestead were generally, but not always successfully, surprised by his subtle enemy; and in pursuit (if the savages were beaten off), the less active European, stood about the same chance of coming up with him, as the slow hound would have in a deer chase; and as far as I can learn from a pretty attentive perusal of the massive correspondence on the subject of the long quarrel between the two races, that is deposited in the office of the Colonial Secretary, filling nineteen awful volumes of manuscript papers, aggressiveness was almost always on the side of the blacks; and in this unequal contest the musket of the Englishman was far less deadly than the spear of the savage, at least five of the former dying for one of the latter. Thus, in the first and largest volume of the series above spoken of, which treats solely of these encounters, we learn that in the five years preceding the close of 1831, 99 inquests were held on such of the white people, whose bodies could be found after death, against 19 blacks, killed in these farm fights; and it is further recorded, that in the same period 69 Europeans were wounded against one, or at most two, of the other race; some of the latter were also taken. That many others on both sides were killed in the same period whose deaths are unreported, is very certain; and equally certain is it, or at least highly probable, that in these unrecorded encounters our countrymen got the worst of it, as they generally did. I have here to remark that the number of inquests actually held must have been much greater than what I have stated, as the coroners of three principal districts were unable to furnish the returns required by the Government, doubtless from the defective state of their office records. I say nothing of the operations of certain bands of whites, called "roving parties," one of which, at least, did kill several of them.

If it had been possible to bring the savage into fair and open fight, with something like equal numbers, all this would have been reversed, of course. But the black assailant was far too acute and crafty an enemy to be betrayed into this style of contest, and never fought till he knew he had his opponents at a disadvantage to themselves. He waited and watched for his opportunity for hours, and often for days, for he knew nothing of the value of time, and when the proper moment arrived he attacked the solitary hut of the stock-keeper with irresistible numbers, or the hapless traveller whom he met in the bush, taking life generally singly, but often; the largest number that I read of his destroying on any one occasion being four persons.

In the assaults on the dwellings of his enemy he contrived his attacks so cleverly as to insure success at least five times in six, and if forced to abandon his enterprise, his retreat, with few exceptions, was a bloodless one.

The natives so managed their advance on the point of attack as not to be seen until they were almost close to the dwelling of their victim. They distinguished between a house and a hut, and seldom approached the former, for they quite understood that there was some difference between the most imprudent stock-keeper, and his more thoughtful employer. They had several instances of this, and profited by their experience. There was no want of pluck in the former, but a great absence of vigilance; and until these barbarians were reduced to a mere remnant by disease and strife, they never attacked except in parties of 20, 50, or 100, or even greater numbers. Their mode of assaulting a dwelling when there were several inmates at home, which they knew by previous watching, was to divide into small gangs of five, ten, or more, each concealing itself as effectually as the clansmen of Roderick Dhu, their approach being so quiet, as to create no suspicion of their presence, to which the woody and uneven nature of the country is eminently favourable. Then one of these parties, which was prepared for instant retreat, made its presence known, either by setting fire to some shed or bush fence, or by sending a flight of spears in at the window, shouting their well known war-whoop at the same time. This never failed of bringing out the occupants, who, seeing the authors of the outrage, now at a safe distance, but in an attitude of defiance, incautiously pursued them ; and no experience of the artifices of the savage, ever taught the assailed a lesson not to continue this insane practice. The blacks then retreated just as quickly as the others advanced, keeping out of gunshot and defying them, generally in good English, to come on ; for it was always found that some of nearly every tribe spoke our language well, as will be presently explained. Having decoyed their pursuers to a safe distance into the woods, and generally with rising ground between them and the hut, the others sprang from their cover, and rushing the place, plundered it of its contents, often finishing their work by burning it to its foundations ; first, however, killing, or leaving for dead, any unfortunate persons—mostly a mother and her children—who chanced to be left behind. They then fled with their booty, reuniting with the decoy party at some distant point.

In their first systematised assaults, which seem to have commenced about 1824, or a little earlier, their principal object was murder ; but in later times, plunder was the chief motive of the savage in attacking the white ; and murder, which was often superadded, only a secondary idea. They took everything that was useful, and often what was no use at all to them ; and more than once afterwards when their encampments were surprised, perhaps 50 miles from any settlement, when instant flight was necessary, they left articles behind that they could not even have known the nature of, such, for example, as clocks, work-boxes, &c., of which there are still extant some curious inventories.

But provisions of all sorts, and, above all, blankets, firearms and ammunition, were the articles they prized most ; of which latter they eventually surrendered many stand to the Goverment —pistols, muskets, fowling-pieces, powder and ball, all perfectly clean and dry, and in excellent order. Of these latter it was found that they knew not only the use, but were practised in using them ; but there is no instance of their bringing them into the field, though they afterwards assured their principal captor and future "protector," Mr. George Augustus Robinson, they meant to have done so, but to the last they seem to have preferred their own arms in both fight and chase—namely, the spear and waddy.

Of firearms they had learned the use from both men and women of their own race, who, having been taken in early infancy by the settlers, were brought up in their own families, mostly as their own children ; but they invariably left them when they grew up, and rejoined their own people, just like woodpigeons, whose natural instincts can never be repressed. To these flights the youths were generally induced by the girls of their own race, with whom alone they could intermarry, and who had, therefore, no difficulty in enticing them into the woods. The natural propensity of the domesticated black females to be with their own people, operated similarly on them, and they became the instructors, in mischief at least, of the wild natives, and strangely enough, were foremost in every aggression on the whites, by whom, with hardly an exception, they had been treated with unvarying kindness, but they were probably thrust to the front by the others ; and, possessed, as the whole race was, of most excellent memories, they never lost the language of our country.

Women, too, who had been either forcibly removed from their tribes, or purchased of their husbands or fathers, by a lawless handful of ruffians called sealers, sometimes escaped from their merciless masters, and after years of separation, rejoined their tribes, and became the most hostile of the enemies of all who belonged to the race of their persecutors ; and notwithstanding the ancient custom of the blacks, not to permit the women to take any part in active war, these individuals could not be restrained from joining in, and sometimes leading the attack. One of these persons, called the Amazon by her captor Robinson, (a woman of one of the East Coast tribes whose real name was Walyer or Taierenore) planned and executed nearly every outrage that was committed in the districts bordering on the North and North-western coast. In the days of their decay, she collected the poor remnants of several tribes into one hostile band, of whom she was the leader and chieftainess ; and true to the natural instincts of the savage, avenged the many indignities she had suffered at the hands of a sealer, on every one she fell in with who bore his complexion, telling Robinson that she would kill the whole race " as soon as she would crush a black snake."

But in their attacks on the widely separated dwellings of the stock-keepers, they were not always successful ; and several instances are recorded of their defeat, and once by the intrepidity of a woman, who held her little fortress for six hours against eight of them (part of a band of 20). The account of this most gallant act is contained in an official report of Captain Moriarty, of the R.N., of the 25th of August, 1831.

Knowing by previous watching that this woman—a Mrs. Dalrymple Briggs—and two female children, were the only occupants of her hut, they abandoned their usual stratagem in approaching it, and advanced undisguisedly to the door. Hearing "some little noise outside," says the report, "she sent the eldest child to see what was the matter, and hearing her shriek, went out herself with a musket. On reaching the door, she found the poor child had been speared. The spear entered close up in the inner part of the thigh, and had been driven in so far as to create a momentary difficulty in securing the child." The savages came on *en masse*, and so quickly, that she had scarcely time to close and barricade the doors and windows before they closed around her dwelling.

Her only means of defence was her musket and a few charges of duck-shot; and their only means of entry, the chimney, which in all bush huts are low, and so large, that two or three persons could jump down them at once. This being the weak point, our heroine took post here, and defied all their efforts to enter, firing her duck-shot at them, whenever they gave her a chance. They next tried to pull the chimney down; but she managed to give one of them such a dose of small lead that they desisted from the attempt. Baffled and repulsed they retired for about an hour, which time they employed in making a number of faggots, and then returned to the attack, to burn her out, as they could not force an entrance. They threw these blazing brands on the roof, to windward, says the report, but she contrived to shake them all off before ignition took place—how, is not stated. Her maternal affections and duties, quite mastering her natural fears, she actually maintained her post against them, for the time I have stated, when an armed and mounted party suddenly galloping up, the siege was raised.

The child that was speared was enticed outside by the blacks, (many of whom were famous mimics), imitating the cries of poultry when alarmed by hawks, &c. Moriarty's report also mentions, that these men had on the same day, attacked the hut of a person named Cubitt, and speared him; and further that the natives had assailed and badly wounded him eight times before; but another report from a different quarter states that he had always been very active against them; and as forgiveness is not amongst the attributes of the savage, nor forgetfulness one of his defects, they never appeared in his neighbourhood without letting him know that they still held him in remembrance.

The craft of the savage and his uniform disposition to treachery, in his early intercourse with the settlers, are very faithfully described in the report of the Aboriginal Committee, 19th March, 1830. This committee consisted of some of the best informed and most intelligent men of the colonies of New South Wales and Tasmania, of whom Archdeacon Broughton, the immediate superior of the church of both colonies, was chairman. From this report I will here make an extract :—

"It is manifestly shown that an intercourse with them on part of the insulated and unprotected individuals or families has never been perfectly secure. Although they might receive with apparent favour and confidence such persons as landed from time to time on various parts of the coast, or fell in with them in remote situations, yet no sooner was the store of presents exhausted, or the interview from other causes concluded, than there was a risk of the natives making an attack upon the very persons from whom they had the instant before been receiving kindness, and against whom they had, up to that moment, suffered no indication of hostility to betray itself. . . . It is within the knowledge of many members of the committee, and has been confirmed by other statements, that even at this period" (they are speaking of the early times of the colony) "there was, beyond all doubt, in the disposition of the aborigines a lurking spirit of cruelty and mischievous craft, as upon very many occasions, and even on their retirement from houses, where they had been kindly received and entertained, they have been known to put to death with the utmost wantonness and inhumanity stock and hut keepers whom they fell in with in retired stations, at a distance from population, and whom there is every reason to believe had never given them the slightest provocation."

This general friendly disposition of the colonists towards them was almost invariably repaid by acts of savage violence ; and they robbed and murdered whenever it was safe to do so. But notwithstanding all this, a kindly intercourse was still maintained with them, and they came to the settlers' houses and departed at will, without molestation of any kind ; until Colonel Arthur, in 1825, wishing to terrify them by such an example as would show them they should not continue their murderous practices with impunity, caused some of the ringleaders and actual perpetrators of a shocking murder at Grindstone Bay, of a person named William Hollyoak, to be apprehended and brought to justice. The offence was proved by some men who escaped from the assault of the blacks, and the murderers were hanged for it ; "after this," says the committee's report, "they came no more to the usual places of resort," and it may be added that they were never more known to visit the house of the settler, or the hut of the stock-keeper except as enemies.

Many of the tribes were united by relationship or other ties, and Colonel Arthur was soon made to understand that the example of these executions had quite the opposite effect to what he expected, for the aggressiveness of the enemy increased ten-fold from the time when they took place.

I have spoken before of the conduct of a few persons called sealers, as ministering to the bad feeling that so long prevailed amongst the natives towards the other race, and I will here say something about them.

These men dwelt on some of the islands in Bass's Straits, and the very worst accounts are given of them by the official protector of the blacks, Mr. G. A. Robinson; and though his statements are very generally confirmed by the prior evidence of some of the witnesses of the Aboriginal Committee, they are not quite so in every particular. Two of these gentlemen, who knew the sealers quite as well as he did, though they loudly denounced the brutality of some of them, accompany their testimony, as to their original possession of the native women, with some slightly palliative circumstances, which he, in his hatred of these men, either overlooked, or was ignorant of.

From the earliest times of the occupation of the country, a horde of reprobates lived on these islands, quite beyond the range of human observation, and equally beyond the controlling power of the Government. They consisted mostly of a mixed class of runaway convicts, of bad character and disposition, and of runaway sailors as profligate as themselves. They lived by collecting the beautiful skins of the seal, which formerly frequented the off-lying rocks of these islands in vast numbers, and are still to be found there, but so greatly thinned are they, and so shy that they are no longer sought after, or not much. These persons often resorted to the coasts of the main land to obtain kangaroo skins, in which they also traded; and if all that Robinson says of them is quite true, they never failed attacking the native tribes who frequented these parts, whenever and wherever they met them, carrying off their women and female children into slavery of the worst description, and shooting the men if they dared to interpose; and he gives such instances of their after cruelties to their captives as can hardly be read with patience. That there was great truth in what he said on this subject is indisputable, for he was quite fortified by the previous evidence of Captains Kelly and Hobbs, who had had accidentally, so to speak, much intercourse with these men in their own various coasting enterprises of discovery, survey, or whaling. But the protector shirks the question of this traffic in women, which the others, who hated these men quite as much as him, impute chiefly to the native men, who first bartered their women for the carcass of the seal or for hunting dogs. These unfortunate women became so useful to their masters, that when they could not get enough of them by purchase they kidnapped them, but made no active war on the blacks until the latter rose against them in a body and killed four of them, "since which time," says Robinson, "the sealers have shot the natives whenever they have met with them." (Appendix, Report 24th Oct., 1830,) These kidnappings contributed largely to the decay of two or three tribes less by their onslaughts on the men than the seizure of the women ; and the protector, in one of his many reports on the condition of the natives, gives the names (mostly unpronounceable ones) of every individual then remaining of two of the tribes, who lived within reach of these fellows, viz.. 74, of whom only three were females ; and two of these three did not belong properly to either tribe, being only visitors.

"This vast disproportion of the sexes," he says, in his report, 20th Nov., 1830, "has been occasioned principally by the sealers, who have stolen their women and transported them to the different islands." And in a marginal note against this passage, he says, "there are at the present time not less than 50 aboriginal females kept in slavery on the different islands in Banks' and Bass's Straits. (Banks' Strait separates the islands he refers to from the main land of Tasmania). But many of these women were, no doubt, obtained by purchase in former years, a practice which in those days was not confined to them, but was universal. But this is a matter that Robinson does not touch on.

To recapture these women and take them under his own protection was always a pet scheme of his, and the means by which he effected it were not always very straightforward or always approved by the Government he served, who made him restore some of them, who, if they were slaves, as he constantly represents them, were the mothers of the sealers' children. No doubt the conduct of these men, like that of other slave-dealers, was very bad, but he seems to have painted it as disadvantageously as he could. Captain Kelly—no friend of the sealer—states that many of the women preferred living on the islands rather than return to their own people, by whom it is well known they were often very badly treated. "The women," Kelly says. in his evidence, "were not always unwilling to go. and after a time preferred stopping on the islands of the straits." He then gives such a fearful account of the torments some of them endured, especially from one miscreant named Harrington, that if they preferred the treatment he describes, to what they underwent from their own husbands, their condition at all times must have been a truly unhappy one.

I learned from Archdeacon Reibey, who visited the straits about eight years ago, that there were then five of these women living on the islands, all very old; but I have since heard that all are dead.

These scalers were never numerous. The protector of the aborigines, in one of his reports, gives the names of all of them living, 29 persons. Their descendants at this day, who are called "the half-castes of the straits" (being the blood of the two races), do not exceed 100 persons.

To put down such an enemy as the aboriginal of Tasmania, who, I have shown, was neither to be easily met with in fight nor overtaken in pursuit, in both of which he so often proved himself the superior man, was obviously a most difficult task; and either his never-ceasing surprises of the settlers must be quietly borne with, or his race must be removed. For a long time the Government *retaliated* with idle proclamations only, published in the official *Gazette* with as much seriousness as if it really believed this captivating journal reached the hands of these barbarians, and were of course only so many contributions to the waste-paper basket of the colony. One of these silly advertisements defined the limits of the districts they were to live in, and directed them in mandatory terms never more to pass the lines described in this terrible order which could not be conveyed to them, nor understood if it were. Abandoning at last this absurd mode of procedure which lasted much too long, while the blacks were devastating the homes of the colonists, almost with impunity, Colonel Arthur took more active measures for the protection of the people, and equipped several "roving parties," as they were called, to beat up the natives' encampments, and if possible to convey to the enemy a message of peace; and as these parties were mostly accompanied by captive blacks, half tamed into subordination, partial intercourse with some of the tribes took place, and beyond doubt it somehow became known to them that the wish of the Governor was to protect equally both races, for when Robinson afterwards got a footing amongst them, he not only found that they were well aware that the desire of the whites was for peace, but that the expiring tribes, who were then dying off almost as fast as they could lie down, were not unwilling to "come in," as he calls it, *i.e.*, to surrender. The dissemination of this desire, in whatever way it reached them, was the principal good done by the roving parties—that is, if it were effected by them, as it is said to have been; though considering what was the practical action of some of them, I should think they did more to increase than allay enmity, and it is more likely they heard it from the civilised youth of their own race, who so often eloped from the guardianship of the settler.—But the tribes still remained as intractable as ever, until a man who spoke their own language, and was master of their various dialects (of which Robinson says there were six), went boldly amongst them, accompanied by ten or a dozen of their own countrymen, whom he had perfectly subdued to his will, and conciliated into affection for his person, and in about five years of most unremitting exertion and toil brought in the whole of them (except about four) who, to the great astonishment of every one but himself, were found not to number more than 250. The causes of this declension I shall explain in their proper place, taking Robinson for my authority. In his various reports he always maintained that this people was nothing but a remnant of the six or eight thousand who were living in 1804, and his reports of their strength he had from the most accurate sources, viz., the natives themselves (who, though they had no words to express numbers higher than four, could repeat the names of the individuals of the tribes, and thus he learned their real force), which he never rated eigher than 700—that is, after 1830 ; and year after year his estimates decreased as they died out, and he then reports 500, and finally 300 or 400, and when he got the last of them they had sunk to the number given above, that is—to about 250.

I hope I shall not be charged with digressing in saying a little about these roving parties, some of whom appear to have wholly neglected their duty, while others quite over-did it. One leader is charged with acting as a land agent whilst in the field, instead of following the blacks—that is, looking up suitable spots for emigrants to settle on for a private compensation ; another with gross improprieties with the half-civilised women of the blacks who accompanied him as trackers and interpreters ; others, with shooting them when they came on the wild tribes—an odd way of delivering a pacific message ; but as some of these charges rest on the report of persons evidently unfriendly to them, they must be read with caution. But when one of these leaders, who was the most active and trusted of the whole of them, tells such a story as the following of himself in an official report to the Government, we have no difficulty in believing that they were not a well-selected set of men for the delicate mission they were entrusted with. He says :—

"On Thursday, the 1st inst. (*i.e.*, September, 1829). I started again in pursuit of the aborigines, who have been committing so many outrages in this district. On Wednesday I fell in with their tracks." These he followed. "We proceeded," he continues, "in the same direction until we saw some smoke at a distance. I immediately ordered the men to lie down, and could hear the natives conversing distinctly. We then crept into a thick scrub, and remained there until after sunset. . . . Made towards them with the greatest caution. At 11 o'clock p.m. we arrived within 21 paces of them. The men were drawn up on the right by my orders, intending to rush upon them before they could rise from the ground; hoping I should not be under the necessity of firing upon them; but unfortunately, as the last man was coming up, he struck his musket against that of another, which immediately alarmed their dogs, about 40. They came at us directly. The natives arose from the ground, and were in the act of running away into a thick scrub when I ordered the men to fire upon them, which was done, and a rush by the party immediately followed. We only captured that night one woman and a male child, about two years old. The party were in search of them the remainder of the night, but without success. Next morning we found one man very badly wounded in the ankles and knees. Shortly after we found another; ten buck shot had entered his body—the man was alive, but very bad. There were a great number of traces of blood in various directions, and I learnt from them we took that 10 men were wounded in the body, who they gave us to understand were dead or would die, and two women in the same state had crawled away, besides a number that were shot in the legs. . . . . On Friday morning we left the place for my farm, with the two men, woman and child, but found it quite impossible that the two former could walk, and after trying them by every means in my power for some time found I could not get them on; I was obliged therefore to shoot them." The number of buck shot that he poured in amongst the sleeping tribe, he says, was 328.

He proceeds to say that he took the unfortunate mother's child from her directly he reached home, sending the mother, herself, to Campbell Town Gaol, of the infant, he says, "I have kept the child, if His Excellency has no objections, I intend to rear it;" and coolly adds in reference to the assault on the tribe. "the whole of the men behaved exceeding well on this occasion." (Report, 7th September, 1829.)

At a distance of little more than a dozen miles from Hobart Town is a large island called Bruny, containing much about one hundred thousand acres, which was formerly inhabited by a considerable tribe of natives. In past years, these people had often committed the usual outrages of the Tasmanian savage on his white neighbour. But this ill-feeling had partly died out through the intercourse they had had with large parties of whalers, stationed for long periods of every year in some of the bays of the island, where they prosecuted, what was then termed the Bay Fishery. These rough fellows, it is well known, cultivated an intimacy with the too facile females of the blacks, conciliating some of the men with presents of food &c., though others were greatly displeased at this intimacy, and indignantly rejected their false friendship; but not so the majority of them. Propriety of demeanour was not uniformly amongst the virtues of the female savage, and very simple acts of good nature propitiated and secured the connivance of, at least, some of the other sex. But all this, though known well enough afterwards, was very little understood at the time. Here, therefore, Colonel Arthur, some time in 1828, formed an asylum for the reception and conciliation of captured blacks, who came in slowly enough, and by ones and twos only. From motives of policy, and possibly of humanity, they were well treated—that is, they were clothed, fed, and hutted, as he meant to set them free again, that they might rejoin their own tribes, and spread amongst them reports of his kindness, and of the friendly disposition of the Government towards them. This he afterwards did, as far as he could; and I quite believe that some good resulted from it, in smoothing the way to their ultimate surrender to Robinson. As for this being actuated by any feeling of compassion towards them, or disposition for "the amelioration of this unhappy race," of which he made such a fuss in his proclamations, letters, and official memoranda, on this subject, I don't believe a syllable of them, or that he cared a rap about them, or what became of them, so long as he could get them into his hands, and thus remove the reproach of their existence at large from the history of his Government. For example sake only, he hanged altogether four of these savages, two at one time and two at another; but when he had the opportunity of punishing any of the very few murderers of this people, he never, as far as I can discover, even censured the authors of this wickedness, his public manifestoes breathing vengeance against any and every body who wantonly molested the blacks notwithstanding, which, I believe, they were put forth for after-effect only. Beyond doubt there were instances of the murder of these people which went unpunished and uncensured. Justice metaphorically represented as blind, was literally so in these cases, and no one stepped forth to avenge the criminality of the white against his sable brother. The cruel act of shooting the two disabled and dying savages above recorded, is a case in point. Far from even censuring the author of this inhuman outrage, he never lost his confidence; but for long afterwards was his trusted councillor in all matters connected with the so called conciliation of "this unfortunate and helpless people," as he was fond of calling them.

Of the asylum at Bruny, Robinson volunteered to take charge—an office more of love than profit—for the consideration of £100 a-year, and a personal ration. He was, by trade, a master builder, but gave up his business, said to have been a lucrative one, for a more congenial occupation, which exactly accorded with the natural tastes of the man. His appointment is dated "March 1829."

He was a person of uncommon energy, and possessed of that indomitable perseverance that never yields to difficulties that the will can overcome. In his many well-planned enterprises, for what he always calls the "subjugation" of the savages, he was often in great danger of their spears; but no risks, however iminent, daunted him for a moment. If they repulsed his advances, or even beat him off, he was at them again next moment. When once on the trail of a tribe, the days, or even the hours, of their liberties were numbered, and their long-known haunts "knew them no more for ever." His heart and soul were devoted to the work of ridding the country of them, without shedding their blood; and when he undertook the seemingly hopeless task, he never doubted his ability to remove every one of them from the main land, which he ultimately effected, with the exception of four, of whose existence he seems to have been misinformed. They must have been reported dead, for at the close of his labours he assured myself who knew him, not intimately, but pretty well, that only one man was unaccounted for, who he believed had died in the bush; and which circumstance I have since seen mentioned in one of his official reports. He was a man of strong common sense, but imperfect education. His first reports, though not badly worded, betray his ignorance of spelling, and also that his grammatical studies were not very complete. But he either improved in these little matters afterwards, or placed his writings for correction in the hands, probably, of a convict clerk, who was subsequently attached to his service. In quoting from these, which I shall have to do rather largely, I shall of course not adhere to his peculiar method of jumbling the letters of the alphabet together, which practice he seems to have learned in the schools of Mrs. Tabitha Bramble or Jeames Yellowplush. He was rather pompous in manner, and vain of his services, in having almost single-handed put an end to 30 years of petty warfare; and his "dispatches," as he invariably calls his interminable reports, in magniloquence of style, throw into the shade altogether the official bulletins of such men as Napoleon, Wellington, and others; still they contain much little known information on very interesting subjects. In his ordinary demeanour he was more patronising than courteous; and somewhat offensively polite, rather than civil. For a long time he quite failed of conciliating the colonists as he had done the savages, and was at first looked on by them as nothing but an impostor; and the flaming descriptions he gave everybody of his friendly interviews with the blacks, which at first had no visible results, were as generally as unjustly discredited.

His first care after taking charge of the new establishment on Bruny Island, was to learn the language and various dialects of the natives; and being a man of excellent natural abilities, he soon mastered this part of his self-imposed work, and thus had a great advantage over all others, as no one but himself knew a word of it; and in a few months afterwards he reports that he had so far got over this difficulty as to be able to converse with them, and that he had commenced the compilation of a vocabulary, which, in the end, must have been a pretty complete dictionary; but I believe he never gave it up to the Government. The language of the tribes seems to have been simple enough, consisting chiefly of verbs, adjectives, and substantives; and from the few authentic translations that have reached us of conversations, &c., a good deal must have been left to the understanding of the person addressed. A couple of examples taken from one of Robinson's long letters will illustrate my meaning. Thus a man whose wife was dying, and to whom he offered food for her, said, "Tea-noailly — parmatter — panmerlia — linener, noaillly," which he translates, "Tea, no good—potatoes—bread —water, no good; meaning," says Robinson, "that his wife had no wish for food of any kind." He gives a portion of a Sunday address that he made to them (for he was an occassional preacher), as follows :—" Matty nyrae Parlerdee, Matty nyrae Parlerdee. Parleevar nyrae, parleevar loggernu taggeerer lowway waeranggelly. Parlerdee lowway. Nyrae raegee merrydy nueberrae. Parlerdee waeranggelly. Kannernu Parlerdee. Nyrae Parlerdeo neuberrae nyrae raegee timene merrydy. No ailly parlevar loggernu tageerer toogunner. Raegorropper, uenee maggerer. Parleevar tyrer, tyrer, tyrer. Nyrae parleevar maggerer. Parlerdee waeranggelly timene merrydy, timene taggathe." Which he translates thus :—

"One good God. One good God. Native good. Native dead, go up sky. God up. Good white man sick looks God sky; speaks (or prays) God. Good God sees good white man no sick. Bad native dead goes down, evil spirit (or devil) fire stops.

Native cry ! cry ! cry ! Good native stops God sky, no sick, no hungering.

The frequent occurrence of all the liquid letters in the few words given above will strike every reader. Their language, which is all but lost, was peculiarly soft; and except when excited by anger or surprise, was spoken in something of a singing tone, producing a strange but pleasing effect on the sense of the European.

Three or four months after his appointment to the charge of the asylum, he volunteered to visit the wild tribes in their native haunts, and to use his best efforts to conciliate them. He says, "I have proposed to the natives that they accompany me on the expedition, to which they appear extremely anxious. They are well suited to such a purpose. Their aptitude to descry objects is astonishing, so much so that where my vision has required a glass, they can distinguish. . . . Their presence would gain the confidence of the other tribes. They tell me how they would proceed. That upon observing the natives they would go to them and would tell them that I was very good,—that they had plenty of bread, potatoes, clothes, and huts to live in. &c."

In his many missions to the tribes, he had always several of his trained blacks with him, and often no others; and strangely enough he never, except once, approached their bivouacs with arms of any kind; and though he generally carried some with him, he always made it a point to leave them at his encampment whenever (after discovering them) he went forward to meet them. This procedure, seemingly so dangerous to himself, and novel to them, appears to have had generally an excellent effect, though there were instances of the contrary—namely, in cases where the wrath of the resentful savage was so inextinguishable and deeply rooted that he refused all intercourse, and would meet him and his party on no other terms than those of mortal strife. In one instance, the natives pursued him most perseveringly for hours, determined to kill him and all his followers; and the escape of the unarmed party was almost more than miraculous. In his flight he had to pass through the densest of forests, with the blacks almost at his heels; and to cross a large and rapid river, bank high with water, caused by recent rains; and though he could not swim a stroke, one of faithful followers, whom he always calls his sable friends, got him through every difficulty, and he reached his camp in safety. This repulse daunted him not in the least degree, for after a very brief rest, he went after them again, and after another parley with them of some duration, in which all his persuasive powers were called forth, two of them swam the river and joined him, and two others came in the same day, and before very long he had the whole of them safe. (I shall presently give the details of this adventure from Robinson's own narrative.) He never fired a shot, or used physical force to a native in his life, and I wish I could add that he is quite free from the suspicion of using deception and making promises to them in the name of the Government, which he should have known could not be kept. It was never quite believed by many of the colonists that he got them all by fair persuasion; this I have heard hinted twenty times or more, and I notice in one of his reports that he pretty well convicts himself of this. He was a diffuse and seemingly careless writer, but no man knew better than he how to frame his letters to the Government so as to leave little trace of error behind him. But in a moment of great and natural elation, just after capturing the very worst and most sanguinary of the tribes, the Big River and Oyster Bay people united, he incautiously lets out the secret of his success. He says, "I have promised them an interview with the Lieutenant-Governor, and told them that the Government will be sure to redress all their grievances." (Report, 5th January, 1832.) On hearing which they gave in without one other word, and followed him rejoicingly to Hobart Town, a hundred miles from the scene of their surrender; from whence, instead of having their grievances redressed, whatever they were, they were immediately consigned to the barren solitudes of Flinder's Island (then a new asylum), where the earthly career of four-fifths of them was ere long fulfilled.

His well-instructed, but unsuspecting sable friends were mere decoy ducks, used by him to bring the wild flight into the net of the fowler; and cleverly did he make them play his game. His black associates numbered amongst them, people of nearly every tribe, and were devotedly attached to him by companionship, and many acts of kindness, which though doubtless spontaneous, served his ultimate ends.

On discovering the smoke of the hostile bands, to which his acute trackers never failed to lead him (except once or twice, when their own fears of their wild brethren so overcame them that they dare not approach until forced on again and again by Robinson), it was his invariable practice to halt his party, and form his camp, where he himself remained, with perhaps one or two of his own race (whom he constantly calls his " Uropeans "), and then sent out his natives to negotiate with them for a friendly interview with himself. After a few hours delay, or at the most a day or two, they returned to him, usually with the good tidings that the natives would receive him, when he went forward, and they met in peace. Their astonishment at seeing him trust himself amongst them unarmed, and unattended by any of his Europeans, and at hearing themselves addressed by the white stranger in their own beautiful language was always very great. These circumstances, coupled with the gratifying promises he made them for their future repose and comfort, completed the work of their subjugation, as he aptly calls it.

He often remained at the huts of these simple-minded children of the forest for weeks together, taking part with them in their hunting excursions and nocturnal sports, which, from previous companionship with his domesticated blacks, he quite understood; all of which was only smoothing the road by which he ultimately led them to the great graveyard of Flinders Island.

These pleasant meetings were not always unattended with personal inconvenience; and once during a three weeks' association with this "interesting people," as he often styles them, they infected him and all his blacks with a grievous fit of the itch, which, no doubt, greatly incommoded the party. "During my stay with this people," he writes, (July 27. 1830), "myself and aborigines became infected with a cutaneous disorder to which the natives are subject."

This friendly interview, of which I shall have to speak more in detail presently, ended in nothing but the establishing of friendly feelings, which, indeed, was all that his instructions at this time permitted. He left them with the best opinions of himself and of the Government he served, which were disseminated amongst all the tribes with whom they were on friendly terms. Presently under the heading of "Legends of our Native Tribes," I shall give some of the most notable of his enterprises against the blacks; but will now proceed to the subject of their

CUSTOMS, HABITS, ETC.

Of the mode of warfare of this people little remains to be added to what I have already said, though I shall be unable to avoid incorporating a few incidental remarks on the subject in some of the passages that follow; for example, in describing their weapons, &c., it may be referred to again.

THEIR DECAY.

It was held by some very intelligent witnesses who were examined by the Aboriginal Committee in 1830, and who had been in the colony from the day of its foundation, that at the time of the first landing of the European settlers the number of savages then in the woods was not less than 7,000, a fact which could not be certainly known, but which might be pretty fairly guessed from the number of known tribes, and a good estimate of their strength. In Robinson's time there were 16 tribes still in being, and he says it had come to his knowledge that several others that were extant 15 or 20 years before he wrote (Report, 27th July, 1830) were extinct then (that is, they were in existence in about 1810 to 1815). On the South Coast alone, he enumerates by name five * that have died out, besides several others in the east, whom he does not name. Of the districts of the north, or the interior, he at that time knew nothing. Many of the tribes that were known to the early colonists numbered from 400 to 600 persons, and if there were 20 or 25 tribes existent then, 7,000 can hardly be an exaggerated estimate. If 500 of these were killed defensively by the settlers, or aggressively by the sealers and bushrangers, we may be assured that it is an outside number. A very few hundreds were made prisoners.

Indeed all reliable evidence, of which there is plenty extant, shows that what they suffered from the whites has been most grieviously exaggerated, and by no one so much, but in general statements only, as by Mr. Robinson himself; for he gives not the smallest proof of it, except in the instance of the sealers, and hardly once names the bushrangers. But he adduces abundant examples of murders by the blacks—the "poor helpless, forlorn, oppressed blacks," as he calls the one race, and the "merciless white" the other—expressions he so often uses, without the least proof of their applicability to either race, that one sickens of their repetition. From all that I can learn, by the attentive perusal of a vast mass of documentary evidence, I do not believe even as many as 500 of them were killed, and about that number made prisoners. Of the assumed number, 7,000, who were in the colony in 1803 and 1804, at least 6,000 must have died at their own encampments, from causes not induced by war, except tribal wars. These latter, taken singly, though not very bloody, produced collectively a large number of deaths. Their rapid declension after the colony was founded is traceable, as far as our proofs allow us to judge, to the prevalence of epidemic disorders; which, though not introduced by the Europeans, were possibly accidentally increased by them. The naked savage soon discovered the comforts of covering, and such things as blankets and clothing were often given them by the settlers, or were distributed amongst them by the Government in large quantities; and in their almost countless hut robberies they never failed of taking away every blanket they found there.

---

* These were the Mo-le-oke-er-dee, Nue-non-i-e, Tur-rer-he-gu-on-ne, Pan-ger-mo-ig-he, and Nee-l-won-ne, which were doubtlessly the names of their districts and hunting grounds.

But of all created animals, the untaught savage is the most imprudent; and he often kept his prize no longer than it suited the idle habits of the wanderer to carry it. Hence, he was wrapped up like a mummy one week, and was as naked as a newly-born infant the next. The climate of Tasmania is also a variable one. True, there is hardly such a thing known as extreme heat or cold, but there are very rapid changes of temperature, from moderate heat to coolness. Cold, in the Englishman's sense of the word, is unknown, except in the high lands of the country, where for five months of the year it is bitter enough, and something like a seventh or eighth of its area, is over 2,000ft. high; and no little part of these high-lying lands is double that elevation, and a good deal more, and, therefore, both chilly and humid. The surface is quite as varying as the climate, hence the general beauty of the scenery. Now any person, whether savage or civilised, who wraps up at one time and goes perfectly naked at another, exposed to very frequent changes of temperature, is certainly not likely to keep long in health, but is assuredly laying the foundation of fatal consumptive complaints, from which (such was the peculiar constitution of the Tasmanian savage) almost immediate death was certain, and whenever he took cold it seems to have settled on his lungs from the first. Speaking of the many deaths occurring amongst this people from this cause, Robinson says, "they are universally susceptible of colds, and unless the utmost providence is taken to check its progress at an early period, it fixes itself on the lungs, and gradually assumes the complaint spoken of, *i.e.*, Catarrhal Fever." (Report, May 24, 1831). Again speaking of the tribes inhabiting the Western districts, he says, "the number of aboriginals along the Western Coast has been considerably reduced since the time of my first visit," that is, at the beginning of 1830, "a mortality has raged amongst them, which, together with the severity of the season and other causes, has rendered their numbers very inconsiderable." (July 29, 1832). I am little versed in the science that treats of epidemic diseases, and cannot therefore explain the processes by which they are spread through entire communities with something like telegraphic rapidity, but it is visible to us all, and therefore requires no verbal proof; and the savage of Tasmania was more than ordinarily liable to its attacks, which, unlike the European, he knew no remedy for, and sought only to relieve his pain by a process far more likely to be injurious than beneficial, namely, the excessive laceration of his body with flint, or glass if he could get it, which, by producing weakness, made death only the more speedy and certain. He had none of the appliances or comforts of civilised life, and succumbed at once. Colds, settling almost instantly on the lungs, sent them to the grave by hundreds ; and no wonder that Robinson found a whole tribe housed in a single hut, for whom a twelvemonth before six or seven were necessary ; and I quite believe that the original cause of their decay lay in their own imprudence, generating fatal catarrhal complaints, from which an European, by proper remedial measures, resorted to early, would easily have recovered. These imprudences were, of course, practised only by a few tribes inhabiting the settled districts, but the consequences, which are of course epidemic, infected all before long.

Many of the tribes, particularly of the Western and South Western Coast districts, which were known to be very strong in numbers, long after the first colonisation of the country, were not exposed to contact with the whites, and yet when taken, they hardly ever consisted of 20 persons, and when larger numbers were brought in at any one time they were always of more than one family.

Of their rapid mortality when under the immediate observation of the protector at Bruny, Flinders, and Hunter's Islands, I have said something elsewhere. But it may not be improper to add that at the last-named asylum, sickness was sometimes induced by the neglect of the Government, which persisted for some months in supplying them with salt provisions (in spite of the repeated and strenuous remonstrances of Robinson), which they hated the very name of, and only ate from necessity, but to which they were too long restricted. The little game there was left on the island, after the incursions of the sealers were prohibited, was speedily demolished by the natives. Of shell-fish, there were few or none hereabouts, and no other fish would any native of Tasmania ever touch ; whether it was natural aversion or superstition is not known, but scale-fish of any kind was as much an abomination to the entire race as swine's flesh to the Jew or Mussulman ; and they would literally rather starve than eat it. In this respect they quite differed from the New Holland savages, by whom it is greatly relished. From some not very satisfactory explained cause, the sheep on the island were not touched. Robinson says they were too young and too small for killing ; but the consequence of restricting the natives to salt provisions was to bring on scorbutic complaints, which terminated fatally in some instances.

TREATMENT OF THE DEAD.

In one of the protector's earliest reports, 12th June. 1829, he gives some lengthy, but very interesting, particulars of their mode of disposing of the bodies of their dead. He relates nothing but what he saw himself, of the death of the patient or patients, and final disposal of their corpse. As nothing can be more simple or touching than his account on the subject, I shall quote all he says about them. The scenes he describes took place on Bruny Island in 1829 :—

"Extracts from my journal.—Monday, May 18, 8 a.m.—Visited the aboriginal family, Joe, Mary, and two children. Mary, evidently much worse, appeared in a dying state. Looked wistfully at me, as if anxious for me to afford her relief. Alas! I know not how to relieve her. Only the Lord can relieve in such trying circumstances. Inquired of her husband the cause of her affliction; he said 'Merriday, byday, ligdinny, lommerday.' (sick, head, breast, belly). On each of those parts incisions had been made with a piece of glass bottle. The forehead was much lacerated, the blood streaming down her face. Her whole frame was wasted. She had a ghastly appearance; she seemed in dreadful agony; her husband, much affected, frequently shed tears. . . . Made her some tea; could not bear the afflicting scene; returned to my quarters; the husband soon following me, his cheeks wet with tears, said his ' luberer, lowgerner un-uence ' (wife, sleep by the fire). Stopped about half an hour. I made him some tea for his children. Asked him if he would take his luberer any. He said, ' tea-noailly, parmatter, paumerlia, lineener, no-ailly ' (tea no good, potatoes, bread, water no good), meaning his wife had no wish for food of any kind. In about half an hour I met him coming towards my quarters with his two children, kangaroo skins, &c. At about a hundred yards distant I saw a large fire. It immediately occurred to me that his wife was dead, and that the fire I then saw was her funeral pile. I asked him where his luberer was. He said, ' loggeenee uence ' (dead—in the fire). Walked to the place; the wind had wafted the fire from her body; her legs were quite exposed (here follow a few illegible words); the fire had burnt out; the body was placed in a sitting posture. While ruminating on the dire mortality that had taken place amongst the people of this tribe, I was interrupted in my reverie by the husband of deceased, who requested I would assist him in gathering who-ee (wood) for the purpose of consuming the remains of the body. My feelings were considerably excited at this—an office of all others I never could have conceived I should have been called on to assist in."

Poor Joe's own turn came in less than a fortnight, and Robinson's journal thus describes his death, and gives this time a fuller detail of the funeral ceremonies of a native.

"Sunday, May 31, 5 p.m.—The sick aborigine requested to have a fire made outside the hut, to which he desired to be carried.

Imagining that this man could not survive long without immediate medical relief, I ordered the boat to be got ready, intending to send him to town. But God's will be done. He expired ere it was ready. These are afflictive providences. In the death of this man and his last wife Mary, the establishment has sustained a great loss. He was kind, humane, and remarkably affectionate to his children. * . . . Last Sabbath he appeared in good health, but his spirits were evidently broken since the death of his last wife. He has left two helpless orphans to lament his loss. I took occasion to converse with the natives on account of the death of his two wives, but they told me they did not like to speak of it." (It is right to say that they never spoke of the dead, nor ever again mentioned their names.)

MANNER OF BURNING THE DEAD.

"I was busy preparing for his departure to Hobart Town for medical assistance, when the groans of this man ceased, and with them the noise of the other natives. A solemn stillness prevailed—my apprehensions became excited—I went out—he had just expired. The other natives were sitting round, and some were employed in gathering grass. They then bent the legs back against the thigh, and bound them round with twisted grass. Each arm was bent together, and bound round above the elbow. The funeral pile was made by placing some dry wood at the bottom, on which they laid some dry bark, then placed more dry wood, raising it about 2ft. 6in. above the ground; a quantity of dry bark was then laid upon the logs, upon which they laid the corpse, arching the whole over with dry wood, men and women assisting in kindling the fire, after which they went away, and did not approach the spot any more that day. The next morning I went with them to see the remains, and found a dog eating part of the body. The remains were then collected and burnt.

"I wished them to have burnt the body on the same spot where his wife had been burnt, but whether because it was too much trouble, or from superstitious motives, I know not; but they did not seem at all willing; I therefore did not urge it. . . . After the fire had burnt out, the ashes were scraped together, and covered over with grass and dead sticks."

While the natives were making the funeral pile, Robinson took occasion to extract from them what their ideas were of a future state, and where they thought the departed went to. They

---

* Another of these Bruny islanders, named Woureddy, had the same good qualities, but they were rare amongst the men, who were very tyrannical.

all answered "Dreeny," that is to England, saying, "Parleevar loggernu neuee, toggerer Teeny Dreeny, mobberly Parleevar Dreeny," (native dead, fire ; goes road England, plenty natives England). From what they had seen of the productions of the superior race, they probably thought there was no happier abode in the universe than England.

He tried to convince them that England was not the home of the departed, and though like some other orators, he talked them down, he did not argue them out of their belief.

It has been often said that they had no idea that there was such a thing as a future state ; but this simple reply shows that, however imperfect their notions were on this subject, they quite believed in a life beyond the grave, or rather after the destruction of the body at the funeral pile. He adds that they were fatalists, and also that they believed in the existence of both a good and evil spirit. The latter, he says, they called Rageo wropper, to whom they attributed all their afflictions. They used the same word to express *thunder and lightning*. He also says that the dying native had a keen perception of his approaching end, and when he knew it was at hand his last desire was to be removed into the open air to die by his fire.

Robinson was a reformer, and an enthusiast in everything, and was too fond of persuading them to put off ancient practices for European customs. I believe he almost thought he could make an Englishman out of black materials. Before long he induced them not to paint themselves, from which, no doubt, they derived warmth ; and he now persuaded them to submit to the burial of their dead, instead of burning them. It matters little in what way the living consign their dead to decay, but he was no respecter of ancient customs, and when I visited the asylum at Bruny immediately after its abandonment in 1830, I saw many grave-mounds there.

In the same report, he says they always retired to rest at dusk, rising again at midnight, and passing the remainder of the night in singing to his own very particular discomfort, as there was no more sleep for him after they woke up. "My rest," he says, "has been considerably broken"—by this disagreeable practice of theirs of night-singing—"in which they all join. This is kept up till daylight ; added to this is the squalling of their children," and here he ends the sentence.

In a subsequent report, August 6, 1831, written after he became acquainted with the hostile tribes, he says that the most popular of their songs were those in which they recounted their attacks on, and their fights with, the whites.

It has been customary to rank the Tasmanian savages with

the most degraded of the human family, and possessed of inferior intelligence only. But facts quite disprove this idea, and show that they were naturally very intellectual, highly susceptible of culture, and above all, most desirous of receiving instruction, which is fatal to the dogma of their incapacity for civilisation. Reasoning from such facts as that they went perfectly naked, were unacquainted with the simplest arts, were even ignorant of any method of procuring fire, and erroneously thought to have no idea of a Supreme Being or future condition, they were almost held to be the link that connected man wtth the brutes of the field and forest.

The aboriginal's wants were indeed so few, and the country in which it had pleased the Almighty to place him supplied them all in such lavish abundance that he was not called on for the exercise of much skill or labour in satisfying his requirements. He had no inducement to work, and (like all others who are so situated) he did not very greatly exert himself. Necessity, said to be the parent of invention, was known to him only in a limited degree; and his ingenuity was seldom brought into exercise. His faculties were dormant from the mere bounty of providence. The game of the country and its vegetable productions would have amply supported a native population ten or a dozen times larger than it ever was. Kangaroos, opossums, wombats, birds, shell-fish, were plentiful, far in excess of his wants. Of fruits there are indeed none worthy the name. But in the vast forests of the country are to be found very many vegetables which, though quite disregarded by Europeans, were relished by the savage; and Robinson in one of his letters speaks of his resorting to their practice of using certain edible ferns, which are so abundant in many districts that credulity could hardly believe it. How they prepared them, or what species they used, he does not say. Indeed the subject of their customs and peaceful pursuits does not seem to have been a favourite study of his, and except their practice of lacerating the sick and burning their dead, which he has been at the pains to describe, we gather very little knowledge of their habits from his letters, except from scattered incidental remarks.

His country lying a little north of a line, mid-distant from the pole and equator, the climate of its low-lying lands is necessarily mild and very agreeable, so that bodily covering of any kind, though prized after habituation to it, was easily dispensed with, and the skin of the kangaroo, so fastened over one shoulder as not to impede the free use of the arms, was enough for the female and her infant, the adult male going generally quite naked. That he was ignorant of any artificial means of procuring fire may be traced to the nature of the woods of his country, which, with hardly an exception, are nearly as hard as whin-stone, and not very inflammable either, so that no amount of manual friction could possibly ignite them. Hence his fire, however he first obtained it, like that of Vesta, was never suffered to die out, it being the province of the women to keep it constantly supplied with fuel when the tribe was stationary, and to preserve it when on the move, by bark torches renewed as required. That he had his own ideas, not very perfect ones, of a good and evil spirit, and believed also that absolute annihilation did not occur with death, we have already seen. He, perhaps, did not reflect much on these subjects, but then he was quite uninstructed, and no state of isolation could have been more complete than his own; so that knowledge of any kind from sources outside his island home never reached him. But when once taught, there never was a people, according to Robinson, who more readily received instruction, or were more eager for it than the savages of Tasmania. School learning was acquired rapidly by them, even the adults. Scriptural truth was taught them both by their protector and a catechist specially appointed to instruct them, and they seem to have understood it, and for a short time it may be said of them, in the language of a sacred writer that they "saw it and considered it well, they looked upon it and received instruction." But of their capacity for civilisation, as explained by Robinson, I shall speak by-and-by.

In stature some of them were tall, and a few were robust; but the most of them were slimly-built persons, wiry and very agile. The features of neither sex were prepossessing, especially after they had passed middle age. Their noses were broad, and their mouths generally protruded extremely. In youth, some of the women were passably good-looking, but not so the most of them; and only one of the many I have seen—the wife of a chief—was handsome. The women however appeared to great disadvantage, by their fashion of shaving the head quite closely, which in 'their wild state was done with flints and shells, and afterwards with glass, when they could get it. The men, on the contrary, allowed their natural head covering, wool, to grow very long, and plastered it all over very thickly with a composition of red ochre and grease, and when it dried a little their locks hung down so as to resemble a bundle of painted ropes, the red powder from which falling over their bodies (which were naturally a dull black colour), gave the naked savage a most repulsive look.

The shoulders and breasts were marked by lines of short, raised scars, caused by cutting through the skin and rubbing in charcoal. These cuts somewhat resemble the marks made by a

cupping instrument, but were much large and further apart.
They never permitted their wives or children to accompany them in their war expeditions, either against the whites or enemies of their own race, but left them in places of security and concealment; and Robinson told me that though their wives went with them in their hunting excursions, they did not allow them to participate in the sport, and that they acted only as drudges to carry their spears and the game; but that the fishing business (for shell-fish only, obtained by diving) was resigned wholly to them. The men, he said, considered it beneath them, and left it and all other troublesome services to them, who, in nine cases out of ten, were no better than slaves. If a storm came on unexpectedly, the men would sit down while the women built huts over them, in which operation, as in all others of a menial nature, the man took no part. To make his own spears, to hunt, fight, and salve himself with his ochreous mixture, were his principal, and perhaps only, occupations.

The huts of this people were the frailest and most temporary structures conceivable. They were often meant only for a night, and perhaps were seldom occupied for a week, though those of some of the west coast tribes were most substantial. Uniformity of design was, of course, quite out of the question; for these hovels were suited to the circumstances of the moment only. Some that I once met with in the Western Mountains seem to have been constructed in a great hurry, and were composed of a few strips of bark laid against some large dead branches that were used just as they had fallen from the trees above. Others that I have seen had, pretty evidently, been occupied for several nights. These were also of bark, supported on sticks driven a little into the ground, and were adorned, according to their ideas of ornament, with several rude charcoal drawings, one representing a kangaroo of unnatural appearance, that is, with its forelegs about twice as long as the hinder ones; another was meant for an emu; a third was also an animal that might have been either a dog, a horse, or a crocodile, according to the fancy of the connoisseur. But the *chef-d'œuvre* was a battle piece, a native fight—men dying and flying all over it. These huts were closed only on the weather side, and perfectly open in front, some large enough for several persons, others less; and the one with the elaborate designs was, I suppose, the residence of a single man, being the least of all.

His spear was a long thin stick pointed at both ends, made of a hard heavy wood, called by the colonists tea-tree. The weapon of the adult was 10ft. long or more, and was thrown from the hand only, with great force and precision, having a range of, I believe, about 60 or 70 yards. Both the throwing-stick and shield of the New Hollander were unknown to him. The only other weapon he used was the waddie. This was made of the same wood as the spear; not two feet long, and thicker at one end than the other. It was held by the thinner end, and was used either as a club or a missile. Used for the latter purpose, it was hurled with awful force and certain aim. When his other weapons failed him he fought with stones, and even with these he was a very formidable opponent. The waddie, however, was chiefly used in the chase.

In fight, the vengeance of the savage was not appeased by the death of an enemy. The mutilation of the body, and particularly of the head, always followed, unless the victor was surprised or apprehended surprise. This was done either by dashing heavy stones at the corpse, or beating it savagely with the waddie. In many of the inquests that I have spoken of in the early part of this paper the deceased were hardly recognisable.

The Tasmanian aboriginal in advancing on an unsuspecting victim whom he meant to kill treacherously, approached, apparently quite unarmed, with his hands clasped and resting on the top of his head, a favourite posture of the black, and with no appearance of a hostile intention. But all the time he was dragging a spear behind him, held between his toes, in a manner that must have taken long to acquire. Then by a motion as unexpected as it was rapid, it was transferred to the hand, and the victim pierced before he could lift a hand or stir a step. This practice and some others of theirs, are, I believe, common in New Holland, and seem to favour the idea of original migration from thence. But they were not of the same stock. There was one very marked difference between the races, the Australian being a straight-haired man, and the Tasmanian a wool-headed.

The hatred of the women for their half-caste offspring has been named before, and I have been told that the New Holland woman has the same aversion. My informant was a gentleman who had resided long in the wilds of Australia, and said that though children of mixed blood were to be met at the encampments of the blacks, he never saw an adult half caste amongst them, and he believed they destroyed them. There are about a hundred of them now living in the Straits, the results of union between the sealer and the savage, many of whom have not only reached adultness but old age. But here the parents lived together in settled life, and the fathers, bad as they are said to have been, were there to protect their children. No doubt the characters of these men have been taken from the worst and most hardened of them. But in Australia I have heard that the union from which these unfortunates are produced is of the most temporary nature, and usually dissolved after a brief intimacy, the care of the offspring of it being wholly surrendered to the mother, in whose charge it seems never to reach even adolescence.

It is nowhere stated, that I know of, that polygamy was practised by the Tasmanian; but as the man Joe, whose death and funeral ceremonies I have recorded, had two wives at the same time, it cannot be said that the practice was unknown to them.

To the other services rendered by the woman must be added the entire care of the children. She carried her infant, not in her arms, but astride her shoulders, holding its hands.

The construction and propulsion of the catamaran, or boat of the native, was also the work of the women. This "machine," as Robinson contemptuously calls it, was only used by the people of the south and west coasts. The northern and east coast tribes, he says, "have not the slightest knowledge of this machine." (Report, Feb. 24th, 1831). The configuration of the north and east coasts—which are not much indented with bays—made it hardly necessary to the people inhabiting them. It was of considerable size, and something like a whale-boat, that is, sharp-sterned, but a solid structure, and the natives in their aquatic adventures sat on the top. It was generally made of the buoyant and soft velvety bark of the swamp tea-tree (*Melaluca Sp.*), and consisted of a multitude of small strips bound together. * The mode of its propulsion would shock the professional or amateur waterman. Common sticks with points instead of blades were all that were used to urge it with its living freight through the water, and yet I am assured that its progress was not so very slow. My informant, Alex. M'Kay, told me they were good weather judges, and only used this vessel when well assured there would be little wind and no danger, for an upset would have been risky to some of the men, who unlike the women, were not always good swimmers, though most of them were perfect. In crossing from South Bruny to Port Esperance, which they sometimes did, the distance is not less than eight or ten miles, and in stormy weather this is no pleasant adventure, even in a first-class boat.

They were great flesh-eaters but not cannibals, and never were; and some of them being incautiously asked if they ever

---

* They were sometimes made of wood, a friend of mine who lately conversed with Trucanina, was told by her that she had been on Maria Island; and on his asking Trucanina how she got there, she replied, "on logs."

indulged in this practice, expressed great horror at it. They never named the dead, and certainly never ate them. Large and small game was supplied them so plentifully, that they had no occasion to resort to the revolting custom.

Their mode of ascending trees after opossums, was to cut small notches in the barrel, just large enough to admit the toes. These were cut with a sharp stone. The labour of making these stepping-places with these simple instruments was such as to cause them to cut them at long intervals, which induced the discoverer of the country, Tasman, to believe that they must be of gigantic stature, which I need hardly say they were not. Their condition in a land of plenty rendered an acquaintance with arts of any kind nearly unnecessary. The fabrication of their simple arms, baskets, canoes, string, and necklaces, I believe, exhausts the list of their manufactures.

Their baskets were made of the long leaves of the plant called cutting-grass very neatly woven together; and the necklaces of small, beautiful shells, iridescent, the purple tint predominating. These shells in their natural state have no great beauty, but after removing their outer coating, their appearance is quite altered. This removal they effected with acids, how obtained in their wild state I know not, but I presume from wood. In their captivity at Oyster Cove, where they made them for sale, they used vinegar. I think a moderate heat was necessary in removing this outer covering, for on visiting their huts when they were preparing them, a woman handed me a saucer of them, which she took from the fireplace.

Robinson's reports are so much taken up with his own personal adventures—sufferings from excessive fatigue, his successes and many disappointments, and complaints of the most annoying red-tapeism of the commissariat and port offices, which were then enough to drive one to the mad-house,—that, as I have said before, he does not tell us very much about their customs, which would have relieved the tediousness of his writings. He speaks a little, incidentally, of their internecine strife, and of the ineffaceable hatred of rival tribes, which he takes credit for having entirely allayed, after their removal to Flinders Island, though I shall show he was not quite successful, and that when his back was turned it was very difficult to keep them from coming to blows. Nor does he say one word about their general assemblies of confederated tribes, which they are known to have held, probably to concert measures relating to war. A curious account of one of their places of meeting is preserved in an official letter, written by Mr. W. B. Walker, dated December 24, 1827, from which the following is taken:—

"Some time since Mr. W. Field had occasion to search for a fresh run for some of his cattle, in the course of which he found a fine tract of land to the west of George Town, in which is an extensive plain, and on one side of it his stockkeepers found a kind of spire, curiously ornamented with shells, grasswork, &c. The tree of which it is formed appeared to have had much labour and ingenuity bestowed upon it, being by means of fire brought to a sharp point at top, and pierced with holes in which pieces of wood are placed in such a manner as to afford an easy ascent to near the top, where there is a commodious seat for a man. At the distance of 15 or 20 yards round the tree are two circular ranges of good huts, composed of bark and grass, described as much in the form of an old-fashioned coal-scuttle turned wrong side up, the entrance about 18in. high, 5ft. or 6ft. high at the back, and 8ft. or 10ft. long. There are also numerous small places in form of birds'-nests, formed of grass, having constantly 14 stones in each. The circular space between the spire and the huts has the appearance of being much frequented, being trod quite bare of grass, and seems to be used as a place of assembly and consultation. In the huts and the vicinity were found an immense number of waddies, but very few spears. The stockkeepers, several of whom have given me the same account, call them preaching places, and state that there are two others, but of inferior construction. one about five miles from the Supply Mills, and the other west of Piper's Lagoon, north of the Western River (now the Meander). One of my informants, who has been much in the habit of kangaroo hunting, says they are places of rendezvous, where the natives keep a large stock of spears and waddies. He described the spears as carefully tied to straight trees with their points at some distance from the ground. He states that he has frequently met small parties of natives on their way to and from the two last-named places, and that the parties that ramble about this part come from thence."

Animosities ran high amongst them, and their quarrels never died out except with the extinction of their enemies. They made long marches to surprise them; and to come on them unperceived, if possible, was their constant object. But it was most difficult to approach them thus, the greatest circumspection being necessary, for such was their vigilance, that it was rare to catch them off their guard; and this difficulty must have been much increased when they became possessed of dogs, of which every tribe had an immense pack, varying from 30 to 100. In a country less abounding in game than Tasmania, such numbers could not have been kept. There seems to have been an hereditary feud between the men of the east and the west, and whenever their captor, Robinson, met them, they were either on the march to meet their ancient opponents, or were returning from a victory ; for I do not recollect a single instance in which they ever acknowledged defeat.

It was not till after his bush labours were over that Robinson took charge of Wyba-Luina (as the natives called their village on Flinders Island) with the designation of commandant. He was nominally so from the first, but his long and frequent absences from it required that a resident manager of the place should be there ; and this office at one time was filled by a gentleman of the name of Nickolls, who appears to have had the greatest difficulty in repressing the illfeeling of the members of rival tribes who were then on the island, who, according to the good old customs of their fathers before them, were always for fighting it out, and settling their little differences in this way. This gentleman thus wrote to the Colonial Secretary on the 9th June, 1835 :—"The greatest drawback to a perfect civilisation is the determined hostility of the Ben Lomond and Big River tribes to each other. The Western natives have attached themselves to one or other of the two tribes, as their inclination led them ; thus virtually making the whole body for the purposes of war to consist of only two tribes. It requires great vigilance to prevent them from breaking out into open hostilities : a very little would set them in flame, they are so very jealous of each other. Upon the arrival of those from town who principally belong to the Ben Lomond tribe, at present rather the weakest in number, I much fear a rupture will take place if extreme caution is not used."

But matters went further than this soon afterwards, and the two parties went out to fight, and were only prevented from doing so by the prudence of that gentleman and his family, who reminded them of the expected arrival of the Governor amongst them (which was then looked for), and how it would displease him to hear of their differences, and so on ; and my informant told me that just at this moment the topmasts of a vessel were seen on the horizon, which it was thought might be those of the brig having him on board (though they were not so), and they desisted. Their march was described to me as a very regular one, and that they stepped pretty well together, singing or shouting some war chant, and rattling their spears as they went along, striking the ground with great force with the foot every third or fourth step. The look of each was determined and ferocious beyond expression. Mr. Nickolls soon afterwards retired from the island, and Robinson, after the completion of his bush services, took charge of the establishment himself.

CAPACITY FOR CIVILISATION.

Of their mental faculties and aptitude for acquiring knowledge he speaks in laudatory terms. In a lengthy report, dated July, 1836, he gives a great deal of valuable information on these interesting subjects, which dispels the long received notion that they were incapable of civilisation; and as this intelligence relating to an extinct race can hardly fail of gratifying laudable curiosity, I shall repeat a good deal of what he says, running the extracts I make into a continuous narrative :—

"The minds of the aborigines," he says, "are beginning to expand. They have more enlarged views of their present situation, and are grateful for the favours conferred upon them. They are volatile in their spirits, and are extremely facetious and perfectly under command. They studiously avoid exciting my displeasure, and appear grieved if they imagine I am in the least offended. The natives are placed under no kind of restraint, but every degree of personal freedom consistent with a due regard to their health, and the formation of religious and civilised habits. The natives are now perfectly docile, and the greatest tranquility exists among them. The mortality that has taken place among the aborigines on the islands may be attributed to a variety of causes, but the following appear to be the chief—the exposed and damp situations of their dwellings, and the frail manner of their construction; their want of clothing, the saline property of the water, and the continued use of salt provisions. The catarrhal and pneumonic attacks to which they are so subject, and which are the only fatal diseases among them, are caused by the injudicious system of changing their food and manner of life.

"The natives are instructed in the principles of the Christian religion. Public worship is celebrated twice on the Sabbath. The service is commenced by singing, and reading from the Scriptures select portions, &c. A short prayer, a few cursory remarks from Scripture are then delivered, when the service is concluded by singing and prayer. The native youth, Walter, acts on these occasions as clerk, giving out the hymns, and reading the responses. The rest of the service is conducted by the catechist.

"Catechetical instruction is the best suited to the capacities of the natives; for which purpose the catechist was a short time since to commence a course of this instruction on Tuesday evenings and which is the only weekly religious instruction afforded the natives.

"In reference to the foregoing subjects, I am proud to state that the most astonishing and marked improvement has taken place among the aborigines. In the attendance at divine worship the people are left in a great degree to their own choice, and which, in matters of religion, I think they ought. But as example teaches before precept, I am a constant and regular attendant. Their conduct during divine worship is of the most exemplary kind. They are quiet and attentive to what is said, and the church is crowded. The ignorance of the natives heretofore in the first principles of religion was more the fault of the system than of the people, for I am fully persuaded they are capable of high mental improvement.

SACRED MELODY.

"This had always appeared to me a delightful part of worship, and as the natives were generally partial to music, I requested singing to be introduced. It is truly gratifying to see with what avidity they listen to this part of devotion. The singing of the women and of the native youth has a pleasing effect, their melody being soft and harmonious.

"My family and the civil officers and their wives act as teachers (*i.e.*, of the native schools), and the average attendance is from 60 to 80. No language can do justice to the intense anxiety manifested by the adult aboriginal for learning, it must be seen to be properly comprehended. The desire of the natives for learning is not the result of compulsion, but is the free exercise of their own unbiassed judgment. Six months have now passed away since the schools were commenced, and there is not the slightest diminution of their number. The same vehement desire continues unabated. The anxiety of the natives for the attainment of knowledge is great. Their proficiency is astonishing. Some are now able to read in words of three syllables. The juveniles are making considerable proficiency in learning, and several are in writing, and have acquired a knowledge of the relation of numbers, and some can add tolerably correctly.

"The aborigines have shown every disposition to become civilised. The men are employed in rural and other pursuits, and the women are occupied in domestic concerns, and for which these people have shown the greatest aptitude, and by their frequent enquiries evinced the strongest desire to become acquainted with the arts of civilised life. Their wild habits are fast giving way. Their corroberies (*i.e.*, violent dances, accompanied by vociferous singing) and perigrinations into the bush are less frequent. They are becoming more cleanly in their persons, and are rapidly acquiring industrious habits. The use of ochre * and grease, to which they were so much addicted, they have entirely refrained from. The women take particular pains in the arrangement of their domestic economy. Their cottages are

---

* The natives called this mineral Lat-teen-er, or Lat-te-win-er. See Robinson's note to Editor of *Courier*, March, 1833.

carefully swept twice a day. The cleanliness, order, and regularity observed by the inmates of the new cottages in the disposition of their culinary utensils, furniture, bedding, would do credit to many white persons. In sewing, the women have made great proficiency. They make all their dresses. The native women provide fuel for their fires, they also wash their own clothes, bedding, &c. The male aboriginals are equally industrious. A road more than half a mile in length, cut through a dense forest in the rear of my quarters, to the beach, as well as cross roads, have been done by them. Several acres of barley, the first grown upon Flinder's Island, have been reaped by them with the assistance of the civil officers, and the facility with which they executed this branch of husbandry was a matter of surprise to every one. The Big River and Oyster Bay tribes, taken collectively, are the most advanced in civilisation, (these and the Stony Creek tribe were the most ferocious and predatory of all the natives), and the western tribes, who occupied a country far remote from any settlement, and, therefore, could not have acquired any previous knowledge of rural pursuits, were equally as ready at reaping as the others. Indeed, their aptitude to acquire knowledge can scarcely be credited.

"The natives now cook their own meat and bake their own bread. The contrast between their present and past condition in this respect is striking in the extreme. In their primitive state their mode of cooking was to throw the animal upon the fire, and when half warmed through, take out the entrails, and rub the inside over with the paunch. It was then eaten. Their mode of cooking now is widely different. They follow the example of the whites, and adopt their practices in everything.

"Their chief amusement is hunting (and it seems they soon extirpated the game). When at the settlement, they amuse themselves by dancing, bathing, cricket, trap-ball playing, and recently they have constructed swings. But the amusement to which they are most partial is marbles. The women join in the dance, and have lately taken a fancy to play at marbles also. I have given several entertainments in the bush, which the officers have attended. These festivities afforded them much amusement."

He concludes an interesting report by saying he believes they have no desire to return to their old haunts and ways of life, and so long as he was with them to keep their minds and bodies in exercise it is very likely they thought but little on the subject of their former wild existence. But I have been told that their natural longing for their own districts afflicted them greatly after his family left the island, and that they often sat for hours looking at the hills of the main land, which in clear weather were visible from Flinders Island. But after years of confinement at the Wyba-Luma settlement, they lost hope and fell into apathy.

After retiring from the office of commandant of Flinders, Robinson settled in the colony of Victoria; where for many years he was chief protector of aborigines. He was a native of London, I believe, and died a very few years ago at Bath, in comfortable, but I understand, not affluent circumstances.

Little more remains to be said of the natives but what is unpleasant to relate.

On the retirement of this most useful and energetic man from the public service of Tasmania, it was difficult to meet with a fitting successor for the office he had filled, and impossible to find one like himself. Such servants are not to be replaced. Persons of better education there were plenty, but who lacked the qualities he possessed in so great a degree, to guide, instruct, and attach the natives to his person. His successors were not of his mould at all, and some of them had no love for anything relating to the duties of their pastoral and paternal office, except its emoluments; and all that he had done for them was rapidly undone. And those who saw the aborigines after their removal from Wyba-Luma to Oyster Cove could never believe them to be part of the same people, who ten years before had given such goodly proof of rapid emergence from barbarity.

A plausible successor of Robinson's, a man of the pseudo dilettante class (a class that flourishes very luxuriantly in Tasmanian soil), probably sick of his isolation, persuaded the headstrong Governor of the colony to transplant the black establishment from Wyba-Luma to Oyster Cove; the worst and most dangerous neighbourhood that could have been selected in all Tasmania. Nothing could surpass the general sterility of the soil of this place (except five or six acres of it) or the moral taint of its atmosphere, its neighbourhood being then inhabited only by woodcutters, who (particularly in those days) contained some of the worst and lowest of our population amongst them. This removal, as I think I have said before, took place in about 1847. Their retrogression was pretty well fulfilled before they quitted their asylum in the Straits, but here their recession into something worse than their original barbarity took place. The apathy into which they had been permitted to sink from neglect of cultivation prevented any recurrence to their old predatory habits, for they had now hardly life and spirit left for action beyond excursions to the public-house whenever they could raise the means, either by the sale of necklaces (or worse practises) or the good nature of visitors. to obtain drink, or as they called it "giblee." Here for several years they were under no other supervision than that of a petty constable or two, and menials, while their paid superintendent was pursuing his elegant studies and follies in Hobart Town, 20 miles off. He was removed from his office, or probably retired, in 1855, but not until the demoralisation of the natives was completed, and the natives had become, when I and many others saw them, nothing better than a horde of lazy, filthy, drunken, listless barbarians; and in everything except the practice of theft, a good deal the inferior of the gipsy.

CHAPTER II.

The history of the old races of mankind furnishes many examples of the decay of nations, but few, if any, where annihilation has followed the declension of their independence, and their emmergence into barbarity. With the subsidence of their power, and loss of national status, they have not necessarily passed away from the earth, but are still represented among its people, though it may be that their descendants are unknown to us by the names that distinguished their ancestors. The many great Communities mentioned in the Old Testament as then existing—the Idumean, Chaldean, Assyrian, and others—though long since politically extinct, have not died off, but are still perpetuated, though not as distinct nations.

The contact of the superior families of mankind with one another, even where it takes the form of collision, does not necessarily imply the extermination of either, and if it has ever occurred at all, it has not been with the frequency with which it has been observed, where civilisation has been opposed to pure barbarism, as in the New World, in Australasia, and Polynesia, where the existence of the primitive man seems incompatible with that of a superior race, as if the approach of the latter carried with it a decree for the retreat and extirpation of the other, though that extinction has always appeared to me, (at least in the case of the Tasmanian savage,) to be traceable to very different causes from those it is usual to ascribe to it, such as the pretended dissemination of European vices and practices among them, to which by far the larger number were never exposed, and to cruelties that were never directed against them in anything like the degree which some inconsiderate writers have too rashly affirmed.

It is not, however, the object of this chapter to repeat what I have said elsewhere, of the real causes that have led to the total eradication of the aboriginal men of Tasmania, but only to collect together before the opportunity is wholly lost, a few of the vestiges that are still unforgotten of a people whose generations have passed away, whose days, as the inspired psalmist says, are gone, and whose years are brought to an end, "as it were a tale that is told."

Of what has been recorded of our first acquaintance with this people, and of their early misunderstandings with the colonists, I shall say nothing here ; nor even follow the fashionable practice of quoting stale governmental proclamations about them (published, as I believe, for after effect only,) libelling the colonists, by describing them as very generally the originators of the many disputes that took place between the two races, but shall commence the task I have cut out for myself by gathering up the few scraps of intelligence I can discover, either of tribes or individuals, of whom any trace is left, who played a part in the outrages that followed the cessation of the partial intercourse that once subsisted between them, and which terminated much about fifty years ago, when it is that their history begins to be interesting.

Up to this time the appearances and some of the realities of friendship existed between one or two of the many tribes, into which the native population was split, and the settlers. But as the favourite hunting grounds of the former were contracted by the spread of settlement, and their occupation by stock, hostile collisions between *black and white* became more and more frequent, and a petty war of assaults and reprisals was carried on, the black people having then, as, indeed, the very generally had the best of the fight. But still this did not put an end to all good understanding, for in some districts both sides continued to exhibit reciprocity of friendship, or, at least, of a civility.

But this intercourse, such as it was, was brought to a close by Colonel Arthur, who was quite as fond of maintaining order by making examples, as of administering the law with strict justice ; and who, managing to catch four aboriginals during the war of attacks and reprisals then going on (each side being as bad as the other,) he, faithful to his practises, hanged them all. The acts, though much applauded at this time of general excitement against the old possessors of the land, have not always found favour with his commentators, one respectable writer, Henry Melville, maintaining that these men, being prisoners of war only, ought not to have suffered for acts justified in war time by the usages of all nations.

With the deaths of these four men the estrangement of the two races, which before was never more than temporary and partial, became complete, and all the fatally disastrous consequences that befell both races afterwards may be dated from these unfortunate occurrences.

But whatever were the sentiments of the white people at witnessing these most impolitic executions, they were viewed by the other race with surprise and horror. At first, however, they did not believe Colonel Arthur to be in earnest with them; for even after the deaths of the two who were first disposed of, they still came to the settlers' homes, and departed peacefully from them as before. But when they saw two more of their number put to death for murder, while no kind of punishment overtook those who inflicted similar violence on them, they sullenly withdrew to the woods, and never more entered the settled districts, except as the deadly enemies of our people.

But in contrast with these and other acts of violence; said to have been indulged in against the blacks, a solitary exception has to be made in favour of one of a most degraded class of men: namely, Michael Howe, the bushranger, of whom it is recorded by the historian of Tasmania, West, that he inflicted severe corporal chastisement on a companion, for wantonly assaulting a native—an instance of commendable feeling, from which his betters might have taken a lesson. The long career of outrage of this outcast, presents too dark a picture to allow us to dispense with one illuminating ray; and I therefore introduce the following extract, from which the above statement is derived, from the *History of Tasmania*, vol. ii. page 17:—"Whether from policy or humanity, Michael Howe formed an exception," (that is to wanton cruelty), "he would not allow them to be molested, 'except in battle,' and he flogged with the *cat* one of his comrades who had 'broken the articles,' by wantonly wounding a native."—*Stated by a companion.*

That the above account of their separation from the colonists is the correct one, is proved by the report of a number of gentlemen styled the Aboriginal Committee, who were appointed by Colonel Arthur, in 1830, "to inquire into the origin of the hostility displayed by the black natives of the island, and to consider the means expedient to be adopted, with the view of checking the devastation of property and the destruction of human lives, occasioned by the state of warfare which has so extensively prevailed," who state, "that after these executions, the natives came no more to the usual place of resort," meaning Kangaroo Point, where the two last who died were taken.

These four men were hanged at different times; two of them, known to the whites as Musquito and Black Jack, on the 25th of February, 1825; and the others, called Jack and Dick, on the 13th September of the next year.

In writing of the origin of the strife that now commenced in earnest, I shall have little to say of these victims, except of the two who died first; for very few particulars have reached us that relate to the others.

The black named Musquito was a native of New South Wales;

but he had resided long in this colony, and was what was called a *civilised black*, that is, one who had lived among Europeans, and learned something of their arts and practises. In former years he had acted for the Government as a tracker of the bushranging classes, then a pretty numerous community, but more particularly as the pursuer of the "last and worst of the bushrangers," as he was styled, namely the notorious Michael Howe. But after the downfall and death of this desperate outlaw, which put an end to freebooting in Tasmania for one long while, his services were no longer required by the police.

It might, however, have been expected that such a person as Musquito, who had "done the state some service," and jeopardised his safety over and over again in his dangerous calling, would have received something more than a mere dismissal when no longer wanted, which was what he got, and no more.

The occupation he had followed so long, and now involuntarily relinquished, acquired for him, especially with the prisoner classes, a large share of the odium that attaches itself to the miserable office of an informer, exposing him to insult wherever he appeared, that was more than the sensitive savage could bear with. Exasperated at the indignities he was doomed to undergo, now that governmental employ and protection were withdrawn, he separated himself from the whites, and joined his fortunes with those of one of the East Coast tribes, afterwards styled the Oyster Bay tribe, of which he became the leader, and, it is believed, its instructor in mischief.

During the period of his connection with these new associates, he is accused of having slaughtered very many stockkeepers; but the number of these atrocities is probably much exaggerated; and the reports, though written in a most inimical spirit, do not seem to implicate him much more deeply in them than the rest of his gang. It was, however, determined to get hold of him if possible, and bring him to justice, that the punishment of such an arch offender might act as a warning to others.

Of the horde with whom the Sydney native was associated, was a man whose tribal name has not descended to us, but who was known to the colonists by the nickname of Black Jack, the same who died with Musquito, as related precedingly. Musquito suffered for the murder of two men, named respectively William Hollyoak, and Mammoa, who was a native of Otaheite; and Black Jack for killing a person named Patrick McCarthy. Jack was also tried for implication in the offence for which Musquito died, as he was present at them along with sixty or seventy others of his countrymen; but as guilty participation could not be brought home to him, he was acquitted of the charges for which the other was condemned. But [McCarthy's death being then brought against him, he was not so lucky as to escape condemnation a second time, and was ordered for execution accordingly.

The murders of Hollyoak and the Otahetian took place on the 15th of November, 1823, on the land of Mr Silas Gatehouse at Grindstone Bay, which is on the East Coast, between Spring Bay and Little Swanport, and about sixty miles, by land, from Hobart Town.

Though not far from the East Coast road, it is even at present a rarely visited and most retired spot; and to any person disposed to encourage despondency, and anxious for complete seclusion and isolation from the world, I should certainly recommend him a location at Grindstone Bay.

There is, however, some fair cultivable land about it, and a large extent of rough pasture ground between the shoreline and the East Coast tiers, which commended it to Mr. Gatehouse as suitable for farm purposes; though what it was that induced anyone to fix his homestead hereabouts fifty or sixty years ago, when nearly all the best lands of the colony were to be had for the trouble of asking, we need not now concern ourselves about. It is, however, as said just above, a grassy tract, and then swarmed with large game, namely, emu and kangaroo, and was one of the hunting grounds of the tribe who were just now roaming about this quarter.

It may be worth remarking that the last emu caught in Tasmania—as far as I know at least—was taken not very far from here, and just about thirty years ago.

But the monotonous quietude that generally prevaded the listless neighbourhood of Grindstone Bay, was dispelled by the unwelcome arrival of a strong detachment of the sanguinary Oyster Bay natives, on Thursday the 13th November, 1823. They numbered sixty-five, and took up their quarters by a small stream that flowed past Mr. Gatehouse's stock hut, then occupied by three persons, namely, John Radford, William Hollyoak, and Mammoa.

But at this period of partial intercourse between the two races, the appearance of a horde of natives, though not an agreeable event, did not always excite the extreme alarm, with which it was witnessed a few years afterwards. But whatever may have been the fears of the solitary stockmen, at the sight of such a number of wild looking fellows, and weird looking women, they were allayed, or partially so, by the assurances of the leading man, Musquito, that no mischief was intended, and all went on friendly enough until the catastrophe that terminated the lives of Hollyoak and Mammoa took place.

The survivor of the rencontre that took place, seems all along to have had some suspicions of the sincerity of Musquito, that were engendered partly by his overacting his part of a friendly visitor, and partly by his everlasting intrusions into the hut, the black eating like a wolf of Radford's provisions, at every visit.

The day before the arrival of the natives, an invalid servant belonging to the establishment of Mr. George Meredith, of Oyster Bay, who was just discharged from the Hobart Town Hospital, and was journeying homewards, arrived at Gatehouse's farm hut; but being still weakly, he was unable to proceed further without a day or two of rest, after travelling sixty miles of one of the worst bush roads in Tasmania. The unfortunate fellow's request was granted directly, and he was admitted. He was William Hollyoak.

The blacks lingered about the premises. unoccupied except when at play, until 2 or 3 o'clock on Friday afternoon, when Musquito and most of his associates went away to hunt, or pretended to do so, but returned before dark, the chief uninvitedly supping with the stockmen of course.

The keen eye of the savage was everywhere, and soon informed him of Radford's means of defence, which consisted of a musket and fowling-piece, which the chief took down from the wall, and examined with the acumen of a connoisseur, and having replaced them, returned to his camp by the creek.

By daydawn of the fatal 15th of November, the blacks were all astir. The principal men of the tribe had by this time taken possession of the stock yard, where they had kindled a fire, round which they sat in earnest consultation, doubtlessly touching the attack they were about making on their white entertainers. The rest of the party, according to the evidence given at the trial, were "over the creek, where they had been at their diversions. The natives who were playing, might be 150 yards from the hut." The stockmen witnessed their games with some interest, and Radford and Mammoa imprudently walked towards them, leaving the invalid at the hut with directions, if he followed them, to bring the guns. He, however, neglected the precaution and joined his friends, which some of the blacks seeing, slipped stealthily inside and secured their weapons unobserved by the three stockkeepers.

The first indication of active hostility was given by Musquito making prize of the shepherd's dogs, and nearly simultaneously by the rest of the natives marching on the hut. On observing the direction they were taking, Radford and Hollyoak ran for their arms but found them gone. By some artifice, Musquito had separated Mammoa from the others, and he re-joined them no more. The natives were at the door directly afterwards, all armed with twelve foot spears except Musquito, who that day carried a waddy only. "They stood" says Radford in his evidence, " with their spears raised and all the points directed towards me and the deceased, Hollyoak," In their defenceless state, the only chance of life left the two shepherds was in flight, and off they set, but pursued by thirty or forty enemies. The first spear that was thrown pierced Radford in the side, and Hollyoak was very badly hit in the back the next instant. At this time Radford was ahead of his companion, but stopped a moment for him and withdrew the spear from his back, and then continued running at a tremendous pace, gaining ground every minute. But not so the other, who was overtaken and speared to death directly, the last words of the dying man that reached his companion being, " O my God, the blackfellows have got me." Radford though speared himself, still ran, and finally escaped them.

The murders of Mammoa and Hollyoak, who were both killed that morning, were accomplished with all the savage brutality usual with the aboriginal man of Tasmania, whose wrath, as said before, was seldom appeased by the death of his victim, and whose body he continued to assault, long after life had gone out. The condition of the corpse of Mammoa is particularly described by the witness who discovered it about eight days afterwards, as having been horribly dealt with—the head beaten almost to pieces—the body pierced by spears in thirty-seven different places, and then thrown into a waterhole; and such was the force with which they cast their weapons at the body that many broken spears were afterwards found scattered about the ground where he died.—(*Gazette*, December 3rd, 1824.)

The principal witness, Mr. John Radford, who gave evidence at the trial of these savages, is still living at Little Swanport, not very far from the scene of the murders described above; and I think I am not far wrong in saying he has resided there ever since—a period of fifty-two years.

Of the death of Patrick McCarthy, for which the companion of Musquito (Black Jack) suffered, no particulars are preserved in the old *Gazettes;* nor of the murder of the stockkeeper, Thomas Colley, at Oyster Bay, for which the other two aboriginals, Dick and Jack, were executed. The *Colonial Times* of the 15th September, 1826, does indeed publish a detailed account of the execution of the two men last-named; but as the article contains nothing very interesting, I shall abridge the details. The elder one Dick, who seem to have had a very lively abhorrence of the executioner, of his entire apparatus, and above all of his office, which he quite understood, resisted the Sheriff's officers most pluckily, refusing to mount the scaffold for any of them; and when forced up at last, he gave them such a specimen of his vocal endowments, as might have been heard halfway to Kangaroo Point; and being a particular sort of a fellow, he would not *stand up* to be hanged, along with the other six culprits (five of them whites,) who were ranked up to die along with him, * but insisted on having a seat, and was accommodated with a stool, on which he squatted himself to receive the final attentions of Mr. Dogherty, the Sheriff's assistant; which seat, says the *Colonial Times* quite gravely, " dropped with him when the awful moment arrived which plunged him into &c., &c. The other black, a mere youth, treated the whole legal ceremonies that intervened between his capture and execution, with great unconcern, but his sufferings were painfully prolonged, by an accident that happened at the moment, before strangulation was completed.

Having described above the origin of Musquito's fleeing to the woods, it is necessary to the completion of his history to explain how he was taken at last.

This man had caused the death of so many stockmen that his removal from his old haunts, and associates, either by capture or death, was no longer a simple desire, but a overpowering necessity. But then to lay hands on a man, so overflowing with artifice and difficult to find off his guard as he, and who was known to be a most desperate fellow, was something like the old project for belling the cat, a thing very easy to propose but difficult to achieve. All sorts of rash designs were proposed by aspiring policemen, or officious *savans* of the outside world, for the capture or destruction of the enemy, that were abandoned as soon as examined, as failures, or sure to be so if tried. However, after a thousand devices had been gravely discussed, with the invariable fate of dismissal as impracticabilities, an idea occurred to a simple tradesman that was worth them all. This man was only a printer and editor—a mere newspaper conductor like yourself, sir.

Mr. Andrew Bent—one of the fathers of the Australian press —was at this time proprietor and conductor of the *Hobart Town Gazette and General Advertiser*, and combined in his own person, I believe, the entire literary and mechanical staff of the *Gazette* office. He was editor—he was reporter—he was reader —he was clerk, compositor, pressman, and deuce knows what besides. He was lame, little, and ugly; but as a counterbalance

---

* At this horrible gaol delivery, no fewer than *twenty-eight* men died. They were executed on four nearly following mornings, in instalments of *seven*, *eight*, *nine*, and *four* persons.

of these personal defects, he was a man of brains, common sense, and industry; and whilst others were propounding all sorts of impracticable schemes for the object above stated, it occurred to him to offer to the Government the services of a domesticated aboriginal youth who was in the employ of Mr. Bent's family as general servant, in the very widest sense of the word, his duties in the house being as multiform as his master's were in the office.

Tegg (such being the name by which the young black was known) is reported to have been a most intelligent lad of about seventeen, possessed of all the artifices common to his race, and above all that acuteness of vision, which, united to practice, made a perfect hunting-dog of him, able to follow even the smallest game by its tracks. This boy had been employed to chase bush-rangers, and on one occasion the gang led by Matthew Brady was dispersed through his co-operation with the police.

Colonel Arthur accepted Bent's offer and according to a pretty broad statement which appears in the *Gazette* of the 8th of April, 1825, promised the boy a boat, if successful, which he greatly coveted. This lad had acquired a notion of trading whilst living with the whites, and Bent says he meant to run her between Hobart Town and Bruny Island, to traffic with his countrymen there in kangaroo skins. But after the capture of Musquito by him, the promise was forgotten, and the keen feelings of the boy were so wounded by this cruel and impolitic breach of faith, that in sheer resentment of it he quitted Bent's employ, and says the *Gazette* quoted from just above, he was heard as he left the house, to say, "they promised me a boat, but they no give it; me therefore go with wild mob, and kill all white men come near me," a true exposition of the savage style of thought, which meditates indiscriminate and general resentment for a single wrong; and he accordingly joined the wild natives, transformed almost in a moment from a tractable youth to a very demon.

The young black, accompanied by two Europeans, named Godfrey and Marshall, all well armed, started from Hobart Town early in August, 1824 *en route* for the usual retreats of the Oyster Bay tribe. All of them must have been excellent walkers; for, notwithstanding the dreadful state of the East Coast road then, they reached Oyster Bay on the third day of their journey, a feat that would not be too easily accomplished even now.

The malevolent angel that had heretofore directed the movements, and watched over the safety of the grim chieftain Musquito, deserted his charge of this moment of danger, and took side with his enemy. For some cause, perhaps momentary caprice only, he was encamped with his two women by himself, the rest of the tribe being in another glen. Tegg had good information of his movements and of the direction he had taken, so he got on his tracks without difficulty. Fatigued as the party were after their rapid march, the pursuit commenced immediately, and before dusk of the day of their arrival at Oyster Bay, they came in view of the bivouac of the savage. He had, luckily, no dogs, and not expecting a hostile visit from anyone, he was not on the watch, as usual with him. His women were at a little distance from the wretched bark weather screen they had put up for him, to break the force of the cutting wind, which was cold enough now. Tegg directed his companions to take post between the chief and his females, which they did by stealthily advancing in the direction indicated by the young black, but who himself made a cat-like movement toward the hovel in which Musquito lay, half-roasting himself by the fire that blazed up merrily in front of it.

Musquito started from the ground at the first indication of approaching footsteps, at sound of which Tegg darted forward to confront him before could seize his arms, which Tegg divined, but for once wrongly, that the other had at hand; but so assured was the doomed man of security, that he had not a spear in his camp. Tegg then fired at him, sending a ball through his body, from one barrel and two into his thighs from the other. But badly wounded as he was he ran off, but pain and loss of blood soon brought him to a stand.

In the meantime Godfrey and Marshall had taken both of Musquito's wives; and whilst the latter stood sentry over the two prisoners, Godfrey ran off to assist Tegg. On joining his youthful leader he found Musquito wounded, as said above, and at bay, but still making a poor effort to defend himself with sticks and stones. Seeing, however, the futility of resisting two armed men, he at length surrendered.

How it was that a man so badly wounded was got to Hobart Town, I have no information, but suppose he was sent round by water. He reached this place late in the evening of the 12th of August, and was placed in the Hospital, where the sable chief was interviewed by his brother potentate, the Governor; from whence, in process of time, he was removed to the Supreme Court, to take his trial for the murders named above, and from here, by a natural transition, to the condemned cell and gibbet.

If the report such as it is, that is given in the official *Gazette* of the trial of this man be correct, it is not easy to understand on what it was he was convicted; for whatever may have been his guilt, there was no legal proof of any, beyond presence at the hut along with sixty or seventy more, and some slightly suspicions circumstances, but not enough, at least, for a jury of our times to convict on, or on which a modern judge would condemn. But as it may have been thought necessary to make a few examples he may have been sacrificed to intimidate his surviving brethren into submission to the superior race ; and from what I remember of the Governor of the time, of the judge who tried them, and of military juries generally, I don't believe that justice, or anything like it, was always done here fifty years ago.

But whatever was the motive that led to these executions, it quite failed of producing anything but evil, its only effect being to imbue the entire race with a most active spirit of resentment that never died out, so long as they remained at large—about ten years longer ; and Colonel Arthur was quickly made to understand by their unceasing hostilities, and most sanguinary aggressions, that a grand mistake had been made, and that he had formed a very false estimate of their real character, if he thought to frighten *them* into submission by any such examples as these.

Before proceeding further with the few tales or legends of aboriginal existence that I have been able to collect together, I shall say a little of the intellectual endowments and martial character of the extinct Tasmanians, stating here once for all that I derive a very great deal of my information about them from the best living authority, namely, Mr. Alexander McKay, of Peppermint Bay, who knew this people intimately when in their wild state—who passed several years of an useful life, either in pursuit of them, or amongst them at their camp fires, and who did so much to aid their chief captor, Mr. George Augustus Robinson to "bring them in," as to call forth from the Government of the day, a special notice of the great value of his services.

Of the mental qualities of no race of men, has a falser estimate been made by nearly every writer on Tasmania than of the ancient possessors of the land. In consequence of the untrue delineation of the character of our natives, made by Hobart Town writers, and others who have copied from them; who knew nothing of the bush or its wild occupants, an idea prevailed which has not yet died out, that they stood almost on a level with the brutes of the forest.

The usual style of this class of writers may be gathered from the following sample of one of them that ¡I extract from a work published in this very city of ours about forty-two years ago, whilst several tribes were still at large ; which work was very extensively read at the time, both here and elsewhere, and has been purloined from often since. This anonymous writer thus expresses himself :—" Perhaps of all creatures that wear the human form, they may be justly placed in the very lowest scale of barbarism;" and he adds, "they live in a state of brute nature." But this was not the case, for they were naturally an intellectual race, with faculties susceptible of very easy culture, as they showed when in their wild state, by the clever manner in which (after a brief association firstly with the half civilised Musquito, and secondly, with some other domesticated blacks, such as Tegg for example, and many others,) they planned all their operations against the Settlers, in which they seldom failed of success; and by the facility with which, when in captivity and under *good* guidance, they received instruction, and accommodated themselves to European habits. They must not be judged of by what we of the present day saw of them in the dark state of their demoralisation at Oyster Cove, where, as at Flinders Island during the last years of their sojourn, they were suffered to sink into a state of degradation, even lower that from which they had emerged.

Forty years and more have passed away since they ceased to exist as an independent race of men; and their frequent hostile incursions into the settled districts, their slaughterings and houseburnings, are well-nigh erased from recollection; but that they were a most mischevious, determined, and deadly foe, is proved not only by a multitude of contemporaneous documents, preserved in the Colonial Secretary's Office, but by the newspapers of the day, that teem with narratives of their aggressiveness, and shew us that even in the days of their decay—chiefly from natural causes—they took life about five times as often as it was inflicted upon themselves, besides committing such devastations on property, as we in these peaceful times can scarcely be brought to understand.

THEIR RELUCTANCE TO KILL A WHITE WOMAN.

Mr. McKay, who knew this people so intimately, relates a circumstance in connection with their manifold aggressions on our people, that has not been published before. Indeed it could hardly be known to any except to one who like him, had lived very much amongst them. But it is so creditable to the great mass of them, that justice to the memory of this people requires that it should not go unrecorded. He reminded me of the fact of our women being sometimes killed by them in the many farm fights in which they were concerned; but he assures me that with hardly an exception the men highly disapproved of it; and that every one of this class of murders, with which the whol race was credited, were really traceable to *two* individuals only both of whom were chiefs, namely, the leader of the Piper's

River tribe, who was named Le-ner-e-gle-lang-e-ner, and Monte-pe-le-ter, the chief of the Big River people. McKay describes the first-named as a miserable little brute ; and he believes his sway over the rest was acquired by his excessive impudence and persistent bullying of them, qualities which we see even in civilised life, place a man too often in front of his betters. The other was a finely made, strapping fellow, " Every inch a king," as poor Lear says.

McKay, whose words I took down as he spoke them, says :— "It is very possible that in the excitement of fight, women may have been killed by other men ; but except in the cases of the above named chiefs, there was no premeditation in the act, for they were naturally opposed to taking the life of a female. Of women slain by Montepeleter, were the two Misses Peters of Bagdad, Mrs. McCasker of Westbury, and several others. Of those killed by the other chief, he now remembers the name of one only; namely, Mrs. Cunningham, the wife of a veteran living at East Arm on the river Tamar. The murder of this last named person led to further outrages on the person of a black, who rated the little chief for what he had just done. This man was a Cape Portland native, but was staying with the Piper's River fellows at the time (this practice of visiting seem to have been quite common amongst friendly tribes), "and when he heard of the death of this woman, he spoke very disapprovingly of it, adding that the men of his tribe never killed a white woman. Greatly incensed at his interference, the chief angrily enquired what business it was of his, who was not one of *his* people ? The two disputants soon got to very high words, when all at once the long named chief seized his spear, and drove it through the Cape Portlander's body, and killed him on the spot."

The poor victim's wife and their child were present at the moment ; and she having a keen perception of what would follow, if she remained even for a moment where she was, snatched up her child and hastened to make her escape from the murderer's presence ; but his thirst for blood was not yet slaked, and he sent a spear after her that struck her on the forehead, but it luckily glanced off without seriously hurting her, and she eventually rejoined the tribe she belonged to.

GEORGE AUGUSTUS ROBINSON.

In continuing these legends, it is now necessary to introduce to the reader a personage once well known to the colonists of both Tasmania and Victoria, who during his residence in this colony, rendered it such great and beneficial services as were not surpassed even by those performed by our third Governor, Colonel

Sorell. This man was George Augustus Robinson, to whom Tasmania owed, but very imperfectly paid such a debt, as none but he could have laid it under, in removing from their ancient haunts, every remaining member, excepting four individuals who had escaped his notice, of the sixteen tribes of natives whom he found still in existence, (for several tribes whom he enumerates had wholly died out before) when he undertook the seemingly hopeless task of transplanting them, firstly to Swan, next to Vansittart's or Guncarriage, and finally to Flinder's Islands. They were truly an aggressive race, and the colonists of Tasmania, caluminated as they have been, were never more libelled than by those scribblers, who have described them as uniformly, or even generally, the assailants of the primitive inhabitants of this country.

In the long warfare that ensued between black and white, after their disconnection, as described foregoingly, the aboriginals, with some, but not very many exceptions, began every skirmish, our own race having generally by far the worst of the fight; and if during the historic age of Tasmania, the blacks diminished from several thousands to a very few hundreds, it was owing far more to sickness than strife that they were thus thinned out—sickness, taking the form of fatal catarrhal complaints, that sent them by thousands to the grave.

Forcible measures having quite failed to subdue, or even seriously to damage these people, or to check their unceasing aggressions, Robinson tried other means with them, namely, pacific overtures and conciliation ; and what could not be effected by the combined action of several thousand armed men, he and they who acted under him achieved, without using violence of any kind ; and in about five or five and a half years (between 1829 and 1834) he succeeded in removing every one of them who were left, with the slight exception named above, from the mainland of Tasmania.

I will now take leave to give the details of some of his many pursuits after them, which he continued to make with the most unremitting perseverance at all seasons, and often under circumstances most adverse to success, for five years, during which the native tribes fell one by one into the snare ; for, beyond doubt, they were the victims of the well-devised and cleverly-conducted artifices of a man from whom they had no more chance of escaping than a fly has when entangled in the web of the spider.

His first enterprise against them, undertaken at the end of December, 1829, was quite an unsuccessful one, and excited nothing but derision, and, of course, increased his discredit with the colonists, who believed him be nothing but a plausible charlatan. He despised their taunts, and replied not a word to one of them.

Several months of apparent inaction, but of real preparation, then followed, and it was not before May of 1830 that he set out again with 18 others, 10 of whom were blacks, to confer with the enemy.

Landing at a place on the South Coast, called Recherche Bay, from an open boat, so leaky that it was with the last difficulty he kept her from sinking with her living freight (all thanks to official red-tapeism), he at once pushed over to a further point called Spring River, from which he started inland with his blacks and three Europeans, the rest remaining with the boat. From here he proceeded cross-country to Port Davey, traversing a mountainous, difficult, and heavily-wooded tract, and reached the great open country beyond, about the 17th of May. This part of Tasmania was then, and still is, a perfect alpine solitude, and he saw not the trace of man till he reached the last-named place. "Here," he says, "a numerous band of natives appeared in sight. On observing my people they fled, setting the heath on fire as they went along." He was anxious to confer with them, but the suspicious savages evaded the desired interview. Sending forward some of his blacks who spoke the dialect of the South Coast tribes, they overtook them, and explained the object of this unexpected intrusion on lands that had never been visited by a white man before, and very seldom since, the coast line alone being known then. Their mission was greatly facilitated by one of the women being related to the stranger blacks, and a long-lost brother of hers was found amongst them. The tribe consented to receive Robinson, and the next day was fixed on for his first interview with the wild aboriginal man of the country; the meeting to take place at a point amongst the mountains, about three miles from his tent. Here he went accordingly with his natives and three armed Europeans. The appearance of the latter with their muskets at once excited their suspicions that his mission was not of the pacific nature they expected, and they broke up and left before he could reach them. From this time he determined never again to go amongst them with arms of any sort, and if possible only with his blacks.

Nothing daunted by this failure, he sent after them again, and his black ambassadors once more succeeded in arranging for an interview, and his first meeting with them took place on the 21st. "The object of my mission," he says, "I fully explained to them, with which they appeared highly pleased. With this people I sojourned for about three weeks, travelling with, and sleeping amongst them around their fires at night, accompanied by a few aboriginals attached to the expedition." (Report, July 27, '30)

"During this visit, one of the women of the party, "he says, "espoused a man of the Nine-nees," that is, the Port Davey tribe, and of course followed him no further.

Soon after leaving the Nine-nees, he visited some other tribes with whom he opened an intercourse in his usual manner. "Several of these," he says,, "evinced a hostile feeling, which was ultimately overcome."

There were persons amongst the natives whom he fell in with on this occasion who had formerly lived with the settlers, and spoke our language well. But they used it only in abuse of him, "making use," he says, "of very scurrilous language." The tribes that these men lived with were, he tells us, the most ferocious of any he visited, no doubt instructed by these "civilised blacks," as this class of natives were not very properly called, and of whom I shall have more to say before I have done with the subject.

I should have said before that Port Davey is situated almost exactly at the south-west corner of Tasmania; and from hence Mr. G. A. Robinson, the native protector, in this expedition proceeded overland to Emu Bay, on the north coast, about 160 miles off, by direct measurement; but in following the tracks of the wandering tribes dwelling in the western hemisphere of Tasmania, his route was so circuitous, and his counter-marches so frequent, that he walked 1,000 miles in all before he reached the bay. How he supported his people during his ten weeks' journey does not appear (for he says the only provision he carried was a little wheat meal); but I presume he roughed it, to use a bush phrase, along with his sable friends, living on kangaroos, wombats, opossums, or anything that came to hand first.

He completed this tedious journey on the 26th July, having sown the seeds of future success amongst more than half the native races, and might have taken pretty nearly as many of them as he thought fit, but he was restrained by his orders, which at this time were to conciliate only. During his absence a general order was issued encouraging the apprehension of the natives, but of this he was ignorant until the opportunity was gone, at least for the presnt.

His next expedition was as barren of results as his first one. He this time traversed the East Coast districts, were large bodies of natives were said to have appeared, but could not get on their tracks, and he returned from his wearying enterprise, to experience new proofs of public distrust in him, by which he was in no way distressed.

He was, however, soon afterwards enabled to give proof of his powers to do as he liked with the natives, and to induce their surrender at his will, or pretty nearly so, now that his instructions permitted him to do so, of which he quickly availed himself.

He went again, unarmed as usual, amongst several confederated tribes living in the eastern districts of the colony, and soon induced 13 of their people to follow him into hopeless captivity, and located them for the present at a temporary asylum, formed at a place called Swan Island, lying off the north-east coast of Tasmania. He learned from his prisoners that they had just returned from an expedition, against others of this unfortunate race, over whom they had obtained a victory, if it may be so termed where only three of the vanquished were slain. These fights often lasted for hours, but such was the dexterity of the savage in evading the spears of his adversaries that they seldom struck him. Without moving an inch from his post, he would avoid a discharge of three or four well-directed spears sent at him at the same instant. By a contortion of his body, a move of his head to the right or left, or raising his leg or arm, he seldom failed escaping them all, any one of which would have transfixed the less agile European with the most perfect certainty.

He remained at Swan Island till the middle of the year 1831, organising his new establishment, roving amongst the many islands of Bass's Straits, quarrelling with their occupants, the sealers, about their women, and boring the Government as often as he could with letters filled with abuse of these men, and sickening details of their cruelties, about which I need say no more than I have already done, except that he would have their women, many of whom he took from them, but they also concealed many, whom he never got; after which he returned to his more proper calling of following the natives of the wilderness.

But during nearly the whole of the year 1831, his successes were inconsiderable. He pursued his prey with his accustomed ardour, but the natives avoided and constantly escaped from him; and the most he effected during the best part of that year was the partial disorganisation of some of the tribes, by the rather unexpected but fortunate capture of two or three of their chiefs.

But he was more fortunate just at the close of this year, and removed to Flinder's Island, on which the aboriginal establishment was now planted, the remains of two once powerful and still very sanguinary tribes, after such a series of marches and counter marches, of trials, hopes and disappointments, which he describes in lengthy detail, as it is quite wearying to wade through, the account of his meeting with them and their surrender being the only portions of two long-winded reports, dated

respectively the 5th and 30th January, 1832, that are worth quoting, and from which the substance of what follows is derived.
In the pursuit of these tribes he was accompanied by a party of 15, mostly blacks, and he fell in with the enemy on the great central plateau of Tasmania, which he crossed and re-crossed times almost without number before he could come upon the active and suspicious tribes he was after. He was at a place called Bashan Plains on the 25th of December, when he saw their smoke under a mountain called the Platform Bluff, which, however, was a long way off. How he knew them to proceed from the fires of the blacks I know not, but he constantly asserts in his writings that his own trackers knew the smoke of a native's fire from that of the white—whether by its volume or what he does not say ; and it seems they were never mistaken.
I pause a moment to say that habit, or the exigencies of their state, had given this race a wonderful acuteness of observation, not intelligible to us. Thus we learn from the report of another of their pursuers—not a very successful one—namely the once well-known Jorgen Jorgensen, that they possessed a faculty for discovering water in situations where no European would think of looking for it, and that these strange places were their favourite camping grounds ; and this it is possible, may on this occasion, have been the key, enabling them to determine whether or not the smoke they saw proceeded from fires kindled by some of themselves, from observing them in a place to which none but their own people would resort.
Christmas Day, of 1831—which must have been a dreary one to him and his companions—was passed on the elevated pasture field of Bashan Plains. It was noticed of Robinson on this day, though he was not much given to fits of dejection, he was rather downcast, the natural effect of langour occasioned by the weariness of an unusually protracted chase after the tribe, whom he began to despair of overtaking. But towards evening of this day, the heart-cheering intelligence was brought him by some of his sable scouts, that the smokes of their camp fires were visible, and that they were in the glens of the mountain called the Platform Bluff. The news once more rekindled the usual ardor with which he always undertook a pursuit, and the march recommenced.
When he came on their footmarks at last, his people—such was their acute knowledge of these faint imprints on the grass, which a European would not discern at all—that they at once pronounced them to be those of the Big River and Oyster Bay tribes united. ("A female," says he, "assured me they were the Big River and Oyster Bay tribes. She knew them by their

footmarks.") He followed on their trail till the last day of 1831, when he says:—"I succeeded in effecting a friendly communication with these sanguinary tribes." But his own dark-coloured friends were so much afraid of the strangers, that it was long before he could persuade them to go over to them. They told him they were quite certain these men would kill them all, and made all sorts of excuses to get out of it; but he would not hear them, and one of them, a chief, ran away sooner than face them. His messengers at length consented to go to them, but quite failed in their mission, and instead of procuring a friendly meeting the two tribes marched in a body to his tent to destroy him. He says:—"In less than half-an-hour I heard their war-whoop, by which I knew they were advancing upon me. I also heard the rattle of their spears as they drew near." It must have been a moment of deep anxiety and fear to all; but the wonderful presence of mind of the man, which never deserted him in danger, now carried him successfully through this awful interview, and the extraodinary negotiation which concluded it.

They were now within about thirty yards of him, with their spears poised for the attack, and they were just about discharging them, when they were completely thrown off their guard, at hearing him address them in their mother tongue. The effect of his words on the minds of these unsophisticated children of the wilderness was magical, and they involuntarily lowered their weapons as if spell-bound; and it is a singular fact that before dayclose, they gave themselves up to him as prisoners, and consented to accompany him to Hobart Town, about a hundred miles off, where thousands of us saw them all a few days afterwards, peacefully encamped on his own premises in Elizabeth-street, just opposite James' Brewery. These people had with them *one hundred* dogs.

In his journey to Hobart Town with them, he placed them under no restraint whatever. He permitted them to leave his camp at will, to hunt or otherwise amuse themselves; but such was the ascendency he acquired over them from the first, that they made no effort to quit him, but slept around his tent every night.

In thus giving up their wild liberty, they were seduced by the fair and captivating promises he made them, firstly of an interview with the Governor, who, he told them, would redress all their wrongs, whatever they were; and secondly, of future support and governmental protection against outrage.

It was an awful day for the natives when they trusted the good faith of the Government, which seized them as prisoners directly they got them, and consigned them to the Straits islands, where in a dozen years or so, four-fifths of them died. But I have been told by one of the very few whom Robinson admitted to intimacy, that he was often heard to speak regretfully about the promises he made them on behalf of the Government, being so faithlessly kept.

He always considered the removal of these two tribes as his crowning achievement, and he speaks of it with a little pardonable bombast. "This," he writes, "is all that remains of both tribes. Tranquillity is, therefore, through the blessing of the Almighty, restored to the colony, and the people are treated as human beings ought to be treated. No restraint in any way has been placed upon them." But this tranquillity was not yet restored, for many tribes remained to be brought in, which he afterwards secured, who, by living more remotely from the settled districts than those just ensnared, had less opportunities of doing mischief than them, but still never neglected to do it whenever they got the chance.

The men he had just taken delivered to him several stand of arms that they had stolen in different enterprises. He says, "previous to leaving the natives' encampment the tribes despatched four of their females for spears, when they shortly returned with three large bundles, and the chief of the Big River tribe took me to a tier of hills, and surrendered to me six stand of firearms loaded, viz :—three muskets and three fowling-pieces."

The attenuated remnants of these once powerful tribes, formerly numbering perhaps a thousand people, yielded, all told, only 26 individuals. Yet were they still as troublesome as in the days of their strength, and committed more murders and robberies, in their decay than they were known to have done at any former period. Like most of their race, they had not suffered much from the hostility of the colonists, nor even greatly from rival tribes, of whom they were generally the masters.

Without going into the general subject of the decay of this race in this place. I may venture a passing remark on the subject of their rapid and remarkable declension, which had been going on for some years before this time, as if the very plague had seized on them. Whole tribes (some of which Robinson mentions by name as being in existence 15 or 20 years before he went amongst them, and had probably never had a shot fired at them) had absolutely and entirely vanished. To the causes to which he attributss this strange wasting away, as coming under his own personal observation, I think infecundity, produced by the infidelity of the women to their husbands in the early times of the colony, may be safely added. This, I believe, was not a mere occasional, but very general failing, amongst the women; and prostitution, all the world over, vitiates the powers of the females, wholly obstructing production. Robinson always enumerates the sexes of the individual she took, and distinguishes between childhood, adolescence, and manhood; and, as a general thing, found scarcely any children amongst them, and quite reversely of the natural condition of our race adultness was found to outweigh infancy in a remarkable degree everywhere. In the present instance his capture was found to consist of sixteen men, nine women, and one child.

The well-known doctrine of Strzelecki that the savage woman, after contamination by the white, is invariably and for ever infertile, is only an amusing fiction, instances of the contrary having occurred, both in New South Wales and Tasmania, in cases where I presume the cohabitation was not a very protracted one. Nor can the decadence I have spoken of be traced to infanticide, at any rate of children of their own blood, of whom the mother was passionately fond; though it seems possible that the peculiar exigencies of their state may have sometimes produced a forced, but certainly most unwilling abandonment of them. Instances of infanticide did, indeed, come within Robinson's knowledge; but then the victims were half castes, whom the savage women both of Australia and Tasmania, is known to have detested. In one of the cases in question a mother suffocated two of her offspring by thrusting grass into their mouths till they died. (Report 13th May, 1831.) In concluding his account of this cruel tragedy, he says:—"The aboriginal females in the Straits do not entertain an equal degree of fondness for those children who they have derived from Europeans, in confirmation of which several facts are on record." And he adds, in reference to these murders "this circumstance is borne out by the united testimony of the aboriginal women of the establishment." (Swan Island). But this subject will be treated of hereafter.

The removal of this horde of depredators and professional murderers, from whom the colonists had suffered more than all the rest, was a very eminent service. It is not indeed easy to understand its value now that the large majority of those who were the objects of their craft and passions have passed away by death or emigration; but any one whose recollections, like my own, will carry him back to the period I am writing of, or who will take the trouble to read through the accounts of the crimes of this people, written at the time, and printed in the early publications of the colony, or preserved in at least a thousand M.S. reports, chiefly from the police magistrates of the territory, will be made to comprehend that the capture of these two tribes was an advantage of the highest order to the community.

The black associates of Robinson received a considerable reward at his instance. I do not know its amount, but it was no trifle, and they were to have it in anything they liked, and Robinson was directed to ascertain in what way they would like it paid them and strangely enough, they, every one of them, chose sheep, and a flock, I think, of 500, but am not quite sure (for I write of their numbers from memory only) was placed on Flinders Island for them. He himself received a gift of £300, additional to £100 already paid him. (Colonel Arthur's order, 14th February, 1832.)

ROBINSON AT THE ARTHUR RIVER.

The five years that he pursued them were years of real toil of painful anxiety and bitter privation to him; but he never intermitted pursuit, so long as he thought one of them remained at large; and though in the end he brought all in but the trifling remnant I have named, he never shed one drop of blood. He visited the encampments of even the most hostile of the tribes without arms of any kind, and in seeming confidence, but doubtlessly not without fear, which he must often have felt most keenly, as on many occasions he was in great danger of their spears; but speaking their language, he successfully negotiated with every tribe for its surrender, and brought all in, either to Launceston or Hobart Town. His services were amongst the greatest benefactions the colony has ever received from anyone; and though like all public men who have disdained to bid for popular applause, he had a host of detractors, still no one who remembers the ever recurring incursions of the aborigines into the settled districts, their well devised onslaughts, their murderings and burnings, which he put an end to, will ever underrate his merits, or assign him any other than a very high place amongst those who have done good service to the country.

I have spoken above of the manifold risks he ran in his missions to the encampments of the blacks But from the following extracts from a letter of Robinson's, that has been kindly presented me by his most intimate friend, Mr. G. Whitcomb, it appears he considered one of the greatest dangers he ever encountered from the natives, was at the Arthur River in the North Western districts, from a horde of blacks, headed by a chief named Wyne, all the details of which are contained in the reports he made to the Government, of this assault upon him, which I shall presently quote from.

West Hunter Island,
October the 4th, 1832.

My Dear Sir,—Little did I imagine when I last addressed

you that I should have been so suddenly called upon to encounter one of the greatest dangers that I have ever been exposed to during the whole course of my long career in the aboriginal service. My escape from the hands of these misguided savages is to me a matter of the greatest astonishment, and almost miraculous.

I trust I am fully sensible of the goodness of God in preserving me amid so very many dangers, more particularly on this extraordinary occasion, which was premeditated, and my destruction at that time appeared inevitable.

I had all along considered that my labour was nearly at an end, being well acquainted with these aborigines from the intercourse that I had with them at the time of my first expedition, from the good effects produced on that occasion, led me very naturally to conclude that I should shortly be able to remove them. From a conviction of this circumstance I had written to Mrs. Robinson, acquainting her that I thought I should be able to spend a part of the summer with my family in Hobart Town, provided that my successes met with no reverse; and although I was sensible that the conduct since pursued towards them had considerably excited them, still I flattered myself that I should be able to overcome this difficulty. This attack was therefore the more sudden and unexpected; from the excited state of the aborigines along the western coast, more time and trouble will be requisite ere they are removed, and although I am persuaded of its being effected, still I know that armed parties could not effect the least possible good. . . . Thrice have I journeyed down the western coast, and thrice have I been successful. It is my intention to visit my family forthwith, either from here or Macquarie Harbour. . . . I have been most shamefully neglected as regards supplies. I have here now upwards of fifty souls depending on me for subsistence, and all that I have received from the commissariat at Launceston is one cask of flour, one bag of biscuit, and one cask of salt beef, and 50 blankets. . . .

I remain, my dear Sir,
Yours sincerely,
G. A. ROBINSON.

To Geo. Whitcomb, Esq., &c., &c., &c.

Several months had elapsed since his last success (over the Oyster Bay and Big River tribes) before he was prepared to take the bush again in earnest. This time he proceeded against the people inhabiting the north-western districts, where the Van Diemen's Land Company have large possessions, as they had at the time I am writing of. These districts were then infested by four tribes, each numerically reduced to insignificance, partly through the ravages of the sealers, but chiefly from causes quite apart from war, except, perhaps, tribal war. These men had made many incursions into the estates of the company, plundering their outstations, and killing their servants, with more than usual impunity, but had received one or two checks lately from a small Government party, acting under a person named Alexander M'Kay, * formerly one of the most active and useful *attachés* of the aboriginal embassy under Robinson, from whom he had shortly before parted in anger, at some neglect he felt he had received at the hands of his leader. This man, when acting under Robinson, had taken several natives himself, and handed them over to his superior. He had also performed other meritorious services, which received no recognition whatever, nor were placed to his account in any manner. He was not a man to bear with this kind of treatment, and refused to remain in his service any longer, and, proceeding to Hobart Town, made a report of his own services to the Governor, who always had a high opinion of him. There was mutual dislike between the master Robinson and the servant M'Kay; and that of the former was greatly increased by the spirited action of the other, and he was very little pleased to hear that, directly after his interview with the Governor, he was placed in charge of a small roving party who acted independently of himself. M'Kay was a resolute, active, and persevering young man, and, perhaps, the best bushman who ever traversed the wilds of Tasmania. He soon effected good service, and took several men of the same tribes whose remains Robinson himself was now in pursuit of, for which he received the complimentary acknowledgements of the Government, that were conveyed to him by the manager of the Van Diemen's Land Company's Estates, Mr. Curr.

Robinson, like the race he subdued, never forgot an affront; and had such a dislike of this useful servant of the government, that many of his after reports teem with abuse of him; and every failure of his own against the tribes M'Kay had visited are ascribed to his rash and imprudent attacks, as he call them on the natives which he constantly asserts had thrown the tribes of this quarter, and those of the whole of the West Coast also, into such a state of excitement, that for a time they would hold no intercourse with him, and refused (like Rachel mourning for her children) to be comforted with his assurances of protection, redress. &c. He magnified the defensive action of this man into a barbarous aggression, and a felling blow that he dealt one of

---

* Now living at Peppermint Bay, D'Entrecasteux Channel.

an attacking party on his hard head with the butt of a pistol, in rescuing one of his company from the fury of several of them who had him down, was enlarged into murder, though the man was only stunned and made prisoner of by M'Kay. The manner in which he assails his old servant, even for years after, shows that forgiveness was not amongst his virtues.

The savages of this quarter were a very pugnacious set of fellows, and had long been the objects of the miscreancy of the sealers, and hated the white race accordingly, and they gave the conciliator of their people more trouble than any others, and never was he and his party in such danger of their lives as now, for which M'Kay gets the entire credit.

Of the four tribes inhabiting the north-west districts, he, with great trouble, removed three entirely, and four adults of the other; which last he calls the Tackine or Sandy Cape natives. They were found to number 23 persons, of whom four only were children; a quarter of a century before their strength was probably 50 times greater. The remnants of the three entire tribes that he now took, laid down their spears to him between the 19th of June and the 15th July, 1832, and the four Tackines came over to him on the 4th of September.

His account of these transactions is contained in two reports, dated 29th July, and 14th September, 1832, from both of which the following extracts are taken:—

"In my communication with the 'Tackine' or Sandy Cape natives, I had to encounter one of the greatest dangers that I had ever been exposed to during the whole of my long career in the aboriginal service. . . . These people came with the avowed purpose of massacring my aboriginal attendants and to have seized upon the women and dogs, and to have returned again to their own country. . . . The first indications of these aborigines were discovered on the 31st ult., (August), between six and seven miles north of the Arthur River. From those traces it was apparent that the natives had returned to their own country. They had been on a war expedition in quest of the people I had removed. . . . On my arrival to within one and a half miles of the river, I halted my people and formed an encampment. Three of the recently captured aborigines, with four of my friendly natives, I sent forward to proceed with all possible celerity, and to omit no endeavour until they had effected a communication, and which they considered they could do without my being present.

"On the 3rd inst., I set out to meet the natives, having the previous evening descried a large smoke, a signal that my natives had got to them, and which had been previously agreed upon between me and them. Conceiving that my presence would give them confidence, I crossed the Arthur River, accompanied by four of the friendly natives (this he did on a raft). Soon after I had crossed, a body of wild natives, well armed with spears, were descried in the woods, and advancing to where I then stood. This was at meridian. On their arrival I proposed to cross the river and proceed to my encampment; but this was objected to, and it was suggested that we should remain for the night on the south side of the river, and that the male aborigines should hunt for game.

"Previous to setting off on the hunting excursion, I distributed amongst them presents of beads, knives, boxes, handkerchiefs, &c., with which they appeared highly delighted.

"At the time I met these people I was unaccompanied by any but my aboriginal attendants, and without the slightest means of protection," (he means fire arms, for his men had their spears). "I sojourned for upwards of 18 hours with them."

He says that during the whole night he was with the Tackines "I was kept in a state of the most awful suspense that it is possible to imagine; for it was not till night set in that I was made acquainted with the extreme danger of my situation. Escape appeared to me impossible, and every moment I expected to be massacred. . . . I was in the midst of them. They slept not, but employed themselves in preparing their spears; some sitting with them across their shoulders, others held them across their knees, while others kept walking about. Their fires were put out, and they sat by the embers. My aborigines kept their fires in for the purpose of watching them, and the better to see their spears coming." (Then follows a little half-poetical bosh about nothing being heard but the "hoarse whisperings" of his new acquaintances, &c., which is not worth quoting.) "On this occasion I deemed it prudent not to evince the least feeling of alarm." So he undressed and lay down in his blanket as usual.

"At the earliest dawn of day, they made a large fire, round which the men assembled, and began preparing their weapons intended for my destruction. At this juncture, one of the wild natives (a relative of one of my friendly aborigines) commenced a vehement discussion, and argued against the injustice of killing me, and asked why they would kill their friend and protector?

"I had by this time put on my raiment. My aboriginal companions were exceedingly alarmed, and on looking for their spears, found that the wild natives had taken them away during the night. . . . In the midst of the discussion I rose up and stood in front of them, with my arms folded, thinking to divert their savage purpose. I said if they were not willing to go with me, they could return again to their own country. Scarcely had I spoken when they shouted their war-whoop, seized their spears, and proceeded at once to surround me. . . . My aborigines shrieked and fled. The natives had nearly encircled me—their spears raised, were poised in the air—the friendly aborigines were gone. At this crisis I made off, although I saw not the slightest chance of escape. I pursued my way rapidly through some copse, winding round the aclivity of some low hills, and took a north-east direction towards an angle of the river, on approaching which I saw one of my friendly natives that had escaped, who, with much trepidation, said that all the rest of the natives were killed. At the same instant she descried the hostile blacks approaching, and in much alarm begged me to hide whilst she swam the river and went to the encampment. To have attempted concealment at such a crisis would have been next to suicide, and looking up (for the river hath steep banks on either side) I saw one of the wild natives looking for my footsteps. At this moment he turned, and I lost sight of him. I saw no chance of escape except by crossing the river—the difficulty seemed insurmountable—I could not swim—the current was exceedingly rapid, and it required time to construct a machine" (*i.e.*, a raft, or catamaran). "The natives were in strict search after me, and I expected every moment to be overtaken. . . . I made an attempt to cross on a small spar of wood, and was precipitated into the river, and nearly carried away by the current. After repeated attempts, I succeeded with the aid of the woman.* When about midway the aborigines again made their appearance, and followed my track down to the river. My clothes were left behind. I then returned to my encampment, where my son and some natives were staying. With these people I returned again to the river, and was agreeably disappointed to find that my aboriginal friends escaped unhurt, and that two of the hostile blacks had joined them. The wild natives had assembled on the opposite bank of the river. Here they continued to exhibit the most violent gestures, and were exceedingly boisterous in their declamations, threatening to cross the river and massacre us.

"From these fugitives I learnt that when the hostile blacks found that I had escaped, they searched the bushes, supposing I had hid myself." He also learned that it was their intention to have killed the whole of the party except the women But for Robinson himself was reserved a special fate, namely, the mutilation and burning of his body, "and my ashes," he says, "made into Ray-dec or Num-re-mur-he-kee (*i.e.*, amulets to be worn by the natives)."

* This woman was Truganini, who is still living.

"My exit from the hands of these savages was so sudden and so unexpected, that with all the vigilance (for which they are so remarkable) they scarcely saw me; and the effect produced on their credulous minds led them to believe that I was influenced by more than an ordinary spirit; to this superstitious notion may be attributed in a great measure the preservation of the people's lives. Failing in their attempt to kill me, they became suddenly dismayed, and the consequences that would ensue as a punishment caused them greatly to despond, on observing which, the strangers that now accompanied me reproached and taunted them. They would not nay-wid-ding-er (*i.e.*, eat much), the num-mer (white man) would return with plenty of pur-da-bar (guns,) and kill them all.

"Whilst at the Arthur River, I entered into a parley with the hostile blacks across the river, and assured them that I had no bad feeling towards them—that I forgave them the attack they had made on my life;" and on giving them his usual assurances of protection, &c., two others swam the river and joined him.

But notwithstanding their despondency and dismay, they were greatly irritated at the desertion of any of their people to the enemy particularly their chief, Wyne, who, "putting himself in a menacing attitude, threatened to come over and murder us." Their terrors of the *nummer* and his *purdabar* had quite subsided, and Robinson had great difficulty, he says, to prevent a collision; and had his presence of mind failed him for a moment, the death of all was certain. But following the native custom, he sent up a a huge telegraphic smoke, as if signalling for the assistance of his whites, on observing which the natives went away, and Robinson was not long in doing the same, only in an opposite direction, with his unexpected prize, and eventually reached the land's end of Tasmania in the north-west, namely, Cape Grim, as quickly as he could reach there, followed by his 27 prisoners, who, it may be safely presumed, had no idea that he was only leading them into captivity, from whence they were never to emerge.

Reaching the Cape, after a march of 40 miles, he immediately transferred his prisoners to some large islands called the Hunters, that lie a few miles off this headland. A sealer's boat was luckily lying at the place, and their removal was effected at once, where they would all have been starved but for the fortunate circumstance of the shores and off lying rocks of these islands abounding with sea birds and their eggs just at this season—chiefly the albatross and penguin. The natives were very partial to birds, and Robinson says that when they were very ill they would often eat one, when they rejected all other food, and here they had an abundance of their most favourite diet.

But death which was now demolishing this people, well nigh as rapidly as he could cut them down, followed on their tracks, and overtook them here also ; and 13 of them succumbed to his shafts within the first fortnight of their landing on the Hunters. The doom of numbers of them appears to have been greatly accelerated by removal from their ancient haunts, and the partial adoption, perhaps too hastily, of European habits. Thus in 1829, when he gathered together a couple of score of them on Bruny Island, 22 of them died between the 12th of June and the 23rd of September of that year, in other words in about 15 weeks. (Report, 23rd of September, 1829.) This mortality was also very rapid at their little village, which they called Wyba-Luma, at Flinders Island, where Robinson says about 250 were landed altogether, of whom 120 had gone to the grave, by the date of his general report on their condition of " July 1836 ; " of the remaining 130 (exclusive of a few births that happened at Wyba-Luma) 46 only were living, on the removal of the establishment to Oyster Cove in 1847, the great majority of whom were young or middle-aged persons when taken and landed there. When I visited Oyster Cove eight years afterwards, April 1855, 30 of this miserable remnant were lying in the little graveyard of the Cove, and at this moment of writing, one only (Robinson's first and principal decoy-duck) survives to mourn over the fall, and possibly to deplore, the active share she had in the ruin of her race.

I have but a few more words to say about the captives on Hunter's Island, and these are only to describe the rapidity of their decay, when sickness seized upon them ; and here again I must quote from Robinson, who was the eye-witness of these death-bed scenes. Speaking first of his domesticated blacks, he says, he is happy to say that they are in a state of " invalescence," for he is fond of unusual words ; but he " regrets to state that the strangers have been subjected to a severe mortality, and out of the 27 of the last removed, 13 are defunct. This dire malady," he says, " had every appearance of an epedemic, the patient seldom living longer than 48 hours after being attacked. All ages and sexes fell victims to its ravages, and they generally expired in a state of delirium. They were all in apparent health when first brought to the settlement."

It would be tiresome to pursue him in his other hard and long journeys, after the residue of the blacks who dwelt either in the interior districts or the west coasts. It is enough to say that in the end he removed them all except four. The last tribe that was brought in was captured by his son G. A. Robinson, on the 28th December, 1834. It consisted of only eight persons.

In reporting this ultimate success of his party, he pledges himself to the Government that the entire native race are removed "with the exception of one individual, who was very old, and in a precarious and sickly state. The entire aboriginal population," he continues, "are now removed, and so firmly convinced am I of this fact that I pledge myself to pay the reward heretofore offered by the Government for all the aboriginals that may hereafter be brought in. The final tranquility of the colony, as regards the aborigines, is firmly established." (Report, 3rd Feb., 1835,) But he was not quite correct, for about nine or ten years afterwards four more were taken, who, there can be no doubt, were the last of them, for the smoke of the savage has been no more seen in Tasmania since.

Whatever the future historian of Tasmania may have to say of this ancient people, he will do them an injustice if he fails to record that, as a body, they held their ground bravely for 30 years against the invaders of their beautiful domains.

Robinson was never the popular man he might have been had he been a little more sociable than he was. There was nothing rude or repulsive about him, but still his manner was not assuasive, and as he cared but little for society, he had few friends. He was moreover an enthusiast in everything that his natural tastes permitted him to indulge in, particularly in religious observances,and was an occasional visitor at the hospital, goal, etc., and sometimes read, and at others gave the best advice he could to the unfortunate occupants of these establishments. But the times were not favourable for such devotional practices as these, nor was the small class of devotees to whom he belonged, treated with much reverence then, and though he was never known to take a part in any dishonourable act, still the current of popular dislike ran so strongly against him, on both sides of the island, that he was almost universally denounced as an impostor, and no terms, however vulgar, were too vulgar if only applied to him. The Government, too, while it affected to applaud him in print, and even to reward his services, was not a sincere encourager of his, and its petty subordinates, with many of whom he had necessary transactions, taking their cue from above, seemed to vie with each other to impede, distress, and annoy him, from no other motives, as I believe, than those that sprang from an illaudable sentiment of jealousy—he and those under him having achieved, single-handed, so to speak, what the Governor and his subordinates, backed by four thousand armed men, had failed to accomplish.

This pitiful feeling, I have read, was once exhibited towards him in a manner that he must have felt keenly enough. It was just after some one of his marvellous adventures in the North, that he came into Launceston so emaciated by privation and overwork, and altogether so wretched, that he might have passed for a pauper, as indeed he appeared to be.

Though both himself and mission were known to the community he was sojourning amongst, the ill-feeling referred to a little above, showed itself unworthily enough just now; and the friendless man might have wandered through the streets uncared for and hardly noticed, but for one gentleman, who, though a stranger to him personally, knew him by repute, and who held very different opinions from others respecting the real character, of the man, and of the great value of his services to Tasmania, which he had the moral courage to avow, whilst he vindicated him and the cause he served from the aspersions of those who affected to treat him, at one time as a madman, and at others as an impostor. Moved by the pitiable condition of the wretched wanderer, he at once offered him and his attendant blacks a home so long as it suited him to remain in Launceston, which Robinson willingly and gratefully accepted, and on every after visit he made to the town both he and his followers were welcomed at the same friend's roof. This gentleman was Mr George Whitcomb.

The service thus feelingly rendered was never afterwards forgotten by Robinson, and to the end of his life he kept up a most friendly correspondence with his old benefactor, under whose roof, as the poet Campbell says, he found

> A home to rest, a shelter to defend;
> Peace and repose, a Briton and a friend.

I am unable to name the time of Robinson's arrival here. I believe he was in humble circumstances then, a poor artizan and probably a steerage passenger, a class whose names seldom appear in the published shipping reports. He was a good tradesman and soon established himself here as a master builder, but he was no designer or architect, as may be seen in the case of his own residence in Elizabeth-street (now No. 168), which was built by himself, or after his own designs, and its present curious roof added in after times under his own direction.

After quitting the service of our Government he received the appointment of Chief Protector of Aborigines in Victoria, on quitting which employ, he retired to England, where he died on the 18th of October, 1866 (at Bath, I believe). He was twice married, and some of the sons by his first wife I hear are still living on some of the islands of Furneaux Group, Bass's Straits.

FABLE OF A WHITE MAN AMONGST THE BLACKS.

There prevailed here at one time an universal belief that a man of our own race was living with the blacks, not only on terms of amity, but as the active abbetor of, and instructor in their hostile operations against the colonists This story which was only one of the many Munchausen-like inventions about the natives, with which public credulity was pretty well satiated at this time, originated with a mendacious witness, who told it to the Aboriginal Committee, of whom I have spoken before.

Information so startling, and yet so probable, when viewed connectedly with the many well matured devices of the blacks for surprising the settlers, which men of such low intelligence as they were erroneously believed to possess, received for a long time a too ready credence, and the Committee hastily accepting the intelligence as a most valuable addition to the evidence they had collected, commended the author, as I have been told, to the Government for a special reward, and which I believe he received. But M'Kay, who often related the report to different parties of natives, says they—one and all—gave the most unequivocal denial to it, and assured him there was not the smallest ground on which to base such an invention. But the story, as some will still remember, had gained such credit with the public, that it was nowhere doubted, and on one occasion it nearly cost M'Kay his life, through his being mistaken for the mythical "white man."

A military, but none too martial settler, had just so far completed a residence on a new location as to make it passably habitable for himself and wife ; and in a placid mood of mind, such as steals over us when quite at peace with ourselves and the world, was making an ocular survey of this conception of his genius, in company with the partner of his cares and troubles, just as a tribe of natives, who approached it by the rear as stealthily as so many cats, had gotten possession of it by the back entry. Having satisfied himself by a minute examination of its front elevation, that everything was quite to his mind, he retraced his steps to take another look at the internal arrangements, but only to find every room occupied by a horde of stark naked blacks, more like demons than beings of this world, as wild as the winds of winter, and armed at all points either for attack or defence. According to their crude ideas of enjoyment, they were very pleasantly occupied in turning everything topsy-turvey, having a general rummage, and helping themselves to what they liked best.

At a scene so portentous as this, the captain very naturally started, a good deal after the manner of Hamlet at the sight of his father's ghost; but his fears being more strongly upon him than those of the Dane, his placidity and pluck evaporated simultaneously, and he dropped his wife's arm as quickly as if she had the plague, made for the garden fence (to which he had secured his horse not ten minutes before) cleared it at one leap like a kangaroo, and next vaulting into the saddle, the fine fellow was off with the velocity of Camilla herself,—or as M'Kay in his half-poetical phraseology says, "he hooked it," so quickly that some of the natives coming out for a shot at him, went in again at observing him quite out of range already.

As he was tearing along like the spectre huntsman and hell-dogs of Boccaccio, he chanced to meet my honest friend M'Kay, who, accompanied by a lot of blacks, was in pursuit of the very tribe from whom the astounded shepherd-militant was fleeing like a march-hare. Finding himself placed, as his disordered imagination suggested, between two fires, namely, the vagabonds who had captured his citadel following hard behind, while another set of villians were coming on him in front, the excessive peril of his situation as he believed it, gave him a spark of that false courage that is generated by despair; and raising his gun, which everyone carried then, he was about sending a shot through M'Kay, but was thrown off his guard by the cool impudence of the latter, quietly enquiring, "What the devil had put him in such a flutter?" An explanation now took place that satisfied the military man he was in no danger from the new comers, and M'Kay who was then a match even for a professional walker, hurried rapidly forward to the rescue of the lady, whom her husband had left in the hands of the blacks. But they were gone; and she was nowhere to be found, an idea naturally arose that they had carried her off, and for a while the worst fears were entertained for her safety.

But enquiry soon brought the fact to light, that after the captain's flight, the clatter of horses' hoofs and the shouts of riders were distinguished by the sharp-eared natives, and the greater part of them made off in a body, but not quite all, a few groups of them still hovering about the premises like disappointed spirits. But directly the coast was thus far cleared and the premises vacated, the lady re-entered them alone, and securing a loaded pistol that her husband had left behind him in his precipitation, she marched undauntedly from room to room, and finally into one of the back ones, of which the window was unglazed, calico supplying temporarily the place of glass. As she entered, she observed the head of a black, who was outside, placed against the temporary weather screen as if he were listening. The unflinching heroine walked straight to it and fired on him, but as might be expected of one of her sex, unaccustomed to the use of arms, missed him, and he fled to the woods.

The horsemen whose advance the natives had heard, now galloped up, and rescued the lady from her perilous positon, and she was eventually restored by them to her recreant husband.

THE DEATHS OF CAPTAIN THOMAS AND MR. PARKER.

In a previous part of this paper, I have had occasion to speak of the frequency with which murder and other outrage was done by the primitive inhabitants of this country on the colonists, and of the savage violence with which they treated any victim who fell into their hands, instances of which came to light almost every week, but particularly at those times when the natives were on the move from district to district, or from the coasts into the interior and *vice versa;* their migrations frequently extending over large portions of the island. These ever recurring instances of slaughter, fire-raising, &c., &c., kept the colonists in a state of constant ferment and excitement such as a few of the present generation can have any conception of; and the conversations of every fire-side related in some form or other to these deplorable acts of the natives, which but for the will of the Almighty in afflicting them with sickness in a very fatal form, might, and most probably would have continued to this hour; for with the advantages they possessed of a most difficult country for an European to advance through, it is not easy to understand how they could have been put down, had the tribes remained at anything like their original strength.

But of all the murders that were committed on our race by this people, none that I recollect caused the same amount of regret and consternation as were felt at the deaths of Captain Bartholomew Boyle Thomas, and his faithful farm overseer Mr. James Parker, who died by the hands of the blacks on the 31st of August, 1831; that is to say by the hands of a detachment of the Big River tribe, then encamped very far away from the river by the name of which they were known to the colonists, namely, at Port Sorell on the North Coast.

Captain Thomas had settled in Tasmania about five years before the date indicated above, landing in Hobart Town from the ship Albion on the 3rd of May, 1826. He came hither as manager of an Agricultural Company that had been formed in England the year before—a season known in commercial history as the *Year of Bubbles*, when all sorts of mad projects that an inordinate thirst for gain could beget, were afloat in England, two of which, that were amongst the least unsound of them, were connected with Tasmania, one styled the Van Diemen's Land Company and the other the Van Diemen's Land Establishment, it was with the last named that Thomas was connected, as manager I believe.

The professed, or indeed the real aim of the Establishment, was the improvement of the live stock of the colony, for which purpose some of the best blood that the ample means of the company enabled them to procure was shipped for this colony, along with a number of farmers and farm-hands, to manage the lands and stock of the Establishment. But the fatality that brought to grief nearly all the companies of 1825, attacked this one also with disaster, but it survived it. The misfortune arose from the death of a very large proportion of its costly blood stock between land and land. Thus of five and thirty most valuable horses shipped in England, only twelve were disembarked here, the rest dying at sea; and much the same thing happened to their sheep and horned cattle.

If I remember rightly, it was the first intention of the manager to take up the large tract of land that the partners were entitled to on the coast of Bass's Straits, nearly opposite to Waterhouse Island, which may be about twenty miles westerly of Cape Portland; but happier thoughts eventually prevailed, and the fine estate of Cressy, by Longford, was fortunately selected instead.

But some disagreement occurring between the partners at home, and the manager on the spot, Captain Thomas, he cut the connection, receiving, as I have read, a good round sum for what he gave up, with which he fixed himself at Port Sorell, on a tract of land he was entitled to, and which he called Northdown; and was the first settler established on the long line of coast between Emu Bay and the western head of the Tamar.

I have here to state that after the death of the gentlemen whose names are at the head of this section, their bodies remained undiscovered for many days, notwithstanding the vigorous but not very well managed search that was made to find them. But they were eventually traced out by the indefatigable Mr. M'Kay, from whose narrative and the newspaper report of the inquest, given in a journal then published in Launceston called the *Independent*, it is that the following sketch is compiled.

At this time M'Kay was employed by the Government, but under Robinson, in pursuit of the natives, and he was just then stationed at the Western Marshes, near to the present Deloraine. In the absence of his chief, M'Kay, was at the head of a small party, amongst whom were one or two blacks. News did not then travel quite so quickly as now, and it took six days for the report of these deaths to reach Launceston, so several days were passed before it penetrated the solitudes of the future Deloraine. As said before these gentlemen were slain on the 31st of August, and M'Kay thinks it was on the 6th of the next month, that he chanced to meet Dr. Westbrook, the same he believes who afterwards practiced in Hobart Town, who was passing near to his camp on this day. The doctor knowing M'Kay and the business he was upon, told him what had taken place, and that up to this time, the search parties who were out had failed to discover their bodies. M'Kay immediately took steps to join in the search.

He started accordingly to the residence of Captain Moriarty, who was a magistrate living on his own beautiful estate of Dunorlan, near the Whitefoord Hills, and about six miles beyond Deloraine, to take counsel with him, and to get whatever assistance the active seaman could afford him. The news of these deaths had just before reached Dunorlan, and at the moment of M'Kay's arrival the Captain was discussing the matter with one of the Thomas' family, a nephew of the murdered man, by whom the intelligence had reached thus far into the wilderness.

As this was the age of bushranging, and also when the natives were very active in the practice of mischief, detachments of military were to be met with in every district into which settlement had penetrated, and there was one stationed in this neighbourhood, whom Moriarty found means of starting to Port Sorell, putting them under the guidance of M'Kay, who was the best bushman in the country, as hundreds could then have avouched as well as myself, who have travelled some thousands of miles with him in past years. Moriarty directed M'Kay to lead the soldiers to the Port straight through the bush, whilst he and young Thomas rode there by the usual track.

On reaching the port, M'Kay found Moriarty already there, and that the usually lifeless district was all astir with armed men, of which every district had either sent or was sending in its quota to recover the bodies, for no one now doubted that both had been murdered. The soldiers were acting under the orders of Ensign Dunbar, who had come from George Town, while the constables and civilians were directed by Moriarty and a Dr. Smith, and such was the number of parties, that camp fires were seen nearly everywhere; and in nearly every direction except (as usual) the right one, men were to be met perambulating the bush through all the hours of daylight; but though it was now ten days since the missing men were last seen, not a trace of them had been found up to this time.

I must now go back to the day of the murders to give the

particulars of some occurrences that took place, it may be an hour before the deplorable transactions which form the subject of this paper were completed.

On the day of his death Captain Thomas accompanied by Mr. Parker, rode down to the usual landing place to superintend the discharge of a large boat loaded with provisions and stores for Northdown that had just before this arrived from Launceston. Two bullock carts followed them to commence the conveyance of the freight to the homestead. The boat was a very large one, and the weight of goods on board amounted to several tons. Near to the boat a large tent was pitched, for the convenience of the boatmen when on shore.

A goodly detachment of the Big river tribe were at this time sojourning at Port Sorell, some of whom were sauntering about the shore, but the greater number stood about the tent of the boatmen, who being well armed caused the natives to be civil enough; for they were a set of cunning fellows, and never attacked at a disadvantage. But each side was on the watch, the one to rush the boat, and the other to entrap the blacks, for the sake of the reward that was offered for all who were brought in alive, which I think was five pounds a head, with a good chance of some Governmental indulgence being added thereto, if the service rendered were considerable. With this view the men gave them liberally of whatever they seemed to covet most, such as tea, sugar, tobacco, and bread, which latter, says one of the witnesses at the inquest, they asked for by the name of "breadlie;" but they were too wide awake for their would be captors, for though two of them entered the tent (most likely only to see whether it were worth plundering) not one of them would trust himself within the boat.

When Thomas and Parker come down to the port, the blacks, though bent on mischief, appeared to be perfectly quiet and friendly with their new acquaintances, which the former who was as guileless and confiding as a child, quite mistook the meaning of. He was one of those kindhearted fellows who never suspect others of being worse than themselves, or of entertaining designs that have no place in their own thoughts. He had long held the belief, that this people were poor inoffensive creatures if left alone, and that the manifold acts of violence done by them were defensive only, and not the result of premeditation, as was constantly charged against them, of which opinions their present seemingly pacific demeanour was an abundant confirmation, as he thought; and he at once took the fatal resolution of visiting their camp alone, with the view of aiding the Government in its so called merciful endeavours, to establish a good understanding with them and thus effecting the conciliation of the two races, which it professed or pretended to aim at, which was something like trying to patch up the long established quarrel between the cats and dogs.

On reaching the boatmen's tent, he enquired of the blacks, (some of whom of nearly every tribe spoke our language, as Robinson was constantly discovering) if there were many others about? to which one of them, holding up all his fingers, replied in passable English, "good many more," (*evidence*). "Captain Thomas," continues the witness, "asked them to take him to them, which they readily agreed to do," in other words, the savages were only too happy to separate him from his party and get him into the bush. Thomas now dismounted from his horse to accompany them; but here Parker, who had none of the *fine feelings*, as they are called, of his employer, and no good opinion of the natives strove hard to dissuade him from engaging in so rash an enterprise as the one he was going on, saying to him—"Surely, Captain Thomas, you are never going to trust yourself with those blackguards, who'll kill you directly they are out of our hearing"; but the infatuated settler was not to be persuaded out of his belief of the harmlessness of their nature, and merely replied, "Oh, they are not so bad as they are represented, I am not afraid, and will go by myself." Parker stood amazed at the indiscretion of the other, but mistrustful as he was of the natives himself, the noble-minded fellow, after a moment's thought, would not suffer him to go alone, so springing from his horse and shouldering his double-barrel gun, he strode after him. Parker was a very robust young man, a little over thirty, and possessed of wonderful resolution, and he had no doubt, armed as he was, of being able to protect his employer against half a dozen of them if they came to blows; but the poor fellow had no idea of the artifice inherent in the savage, and in this one particular they were an overmatch for him.

Before following Thomas, he gave a few hasty directions to the bullock drivers, not to start until they returned, which he hoped would not be long first; and on parting from them—as it proved for ever—he ordered them not on any account to let their horses get astray, as they should want them directly they came back.

As Thomas and himself proceeded towards the camp of the blacks, their two or three attendants were, as if by pre-arrangement, soon reinforced by others; one fellow meeting them here, another a little further on, and a third, fourth, fifth, and sixth, somewhere else, until they grew like Falstaff's recruits into a large but most disreputable looking troop, of whom the majority kept an eye on the unarmed captain, whilst two or three only, but the most resolute of their number, marched on either side of his companion, of whom the most conspicuous were two named Mac-a-mee and Wow-ee, by whom the assault that followed was commenced; the former, unarmed, walking on the right, and the other, bearing a heavy waddy, on the left hand.

The party had moved forward about two miles when the assault commenced, by Mac-a-mee, as quick as thought, snatching the gun out of Parker's hand, which he did with such force as to turn him more than half round, and then running off as fast as he could with the prize. At this moment Parker's face was turned away from the other savage, who swinging his waddy aloft, dealt him such a blow on his temple, that he reeled and fell to the ground, apparently a lifeless man.

It is not in the power of language to describe the excitement of the men of the tribe at witnessing the fall of another of the enemies of their race, nor the scene that took place at this moment between them and their wives, such as no one would expect to read of as an usual incident in savage life, the men rushing up with yells of savage joy to finish the fallen man, and the women equally vociferous, interposing, by entreaty, to stay the wrath of their husbands, and to save him from death, but without effect in the case of either victim, and it is a fact that on finding themselves powerless to prevent murder they sullenly withdrew from the scene, neither threat nor persuasion availing to recall them; and without thought of the danger they ran in exposing themselves at such a moment to the whites, they marched in a body to Northdown, where, as will be presently seen they were made prisoners of, as well as some of the men, namely, Mac-a-mee, Wow-ee, and Calamarowenee, who followed them thither to force them to return, but which the poor creatures refused to do.

In the end, Parker was literally nailed to the ground by the spears of the blacks, twelve of which were driven through and through him, every wound, according to the testimony of Dr. Smith, being quite sufficient to cause death.

Captain Thomas, on seeing the fate of his friend, to whom he could give no assistance, ran off, screaming out *murder* as loudly as he could, which the natives, who were often capital mimics, afterwards told M'Kay of, without knowing what he meant by it. He was an uncommonly active man, and on fair ground ran with such speed that few could contend against But swift-footed as he was, he was no match here for the agile savage unencumbered by clothes; and several young fellows starting after him were at his heels by the time he had got sixty yards, which was the distance he ran when they overhauled him. The captain wore a half military frock coat at the time, at the skirt of which the foremost of them made a grasp, and, though it gave way, his speed was so checked that they had him before he could advance another yard. He was knocked over directly and speared to death, his body being pierced quite through in ten places.

The demeanour of the women at this time, as it is described above, was only what they always displayed on occasions like this. They were seldom present at a fight, unless it were an unexpected one, being always left behind, as many have thought, for their safety, but really because their presence was embarrassing to their husbands. for, with rare exceptions, they were against excessive violence being done, and it would not be difficult to give instances where their interposition in stopping it was more successful than it was at this time.

We must now go back to the beach, where we left the two carters, whom Parker had directed to remain, until Captain Thomas and himself returned to them, and where they awaited until the sun was getting low, loitering about till the last minute, so as not to go without them, and firing their guns for their return but to no purpose, for they were both dead long before this; so yoking up their bullocks, they reluctantly faced homewards, taking with them the two horses of the now missing men.

By the time the drivers had got about half way to Northdown they were joined by the black women, who had quitted the tribe after the murders described above, and now followed the carts as though they were of the party. But they had not gone far before they were overtaken by the three men named a little above, who seemed by their gestures, to insist upon their immediate return to the camp; but they were too much excited by the events of the day to obey, so they continued to follow the bullock carts, the three men walking with them, sometimes entreating them to return, and at others threatening them with their waddies if they persisted in going on; but they were not in any temper to do the bidding of the others, and sullenly kept on their way with the drivers.

It was night when they reached Northdown, and as the blacks seldom travelled after dark, there was no help for it, but for all of them to remain at the homestead; and Mrs. Parker, though very little pleased at her husband's absence, having at present no serious fears for his safety, kindly directed the men to look after the wants of these most unexpected, and none too welcome visitors; and she further instructed four of the servants to go to the port at daylight, and, if possible, to trace out the whereabouts of her husband and his employer; and then commenced the wearisome search that followed, and which, but for M'Kay (as I gather from the newspapers of the time), would have proved an unavailing one.

Next morning four of Thomas' *assigned servants*, as convicts in private employ were called, started on their mission ; but not so the natives, the females of whom were still as sulky as black cockatoos are sometimes said to be, and would not return to their tribe ; and as the men would not go without them, about a third of their number were billited at Northdown for two or three days, poor Mrs. Parker entertaining, but most unconsciously, the very individuals who had made her a widow.

The natives had not been long at Northdown, before some of Thomas' men, who began to suspect that foul play had been done, commenced making enquiries of such of the blacks as could understand them, where they had left the gentlemen whom everyone now felt anxious to hear something about. But though it was evident enough there was some misunderstanding amongst them, there was no getting them to play false to each other, and not a word could be extracted from them that the tribe knew anything about them ; but this was not believed, so some of the farm servants, taking the law into their own hands, no uncommon practice with the blacks at that time, enticed them into the most secure room of the house, locked them up, set a sentry over them, and there kept them until the boat returned to Launceston, when they were all marched down to the beach, put on board and sent off to George Town gaol, which wretched place chancing to be empty at the time, they had it all to themselves.

As said before, the search was kept up from morning to night for many days, but neither Thomas nor Parker turned up. though it was now the 9th of September, or ten days after they were missed. Then it was that M'Kay with his soldiers and one native woman arrived at Port Sorell to aid the searchers. This woman whose tribal name M'Kay forgets, was known to our people as *Black Sal*, and like all the women whom Robinson instructed to assist him in the subjugation of her race, her whole heart and soul were in the business in hand. Like the still living Trucanini, she was one of the most artful and energetic of the decoy ducks whom he had trained to entrap the rest.

M'Kay, with the practised eye of a bushman,' had not been long on the ground without seeing that the search was an ill-managed one, prosecuted by men of slight bush experience only, who instead of *finding* anyone, were constantly getting *lost themselves*. and that unless some other means were employed to discover the missing men or their remains, the entire plan must end in failure.

M'Kay *is*, what poor Moriarty *was*, a [...] born sailor, and being known to the Captain, had his confidence ; and he now suggested the surest way to succeed was for himsel[f] to proceed directly to George Town, along with his companic[...] n Black Sal, to confer with the imprisoned natives ; explaining to the Captain, that as he spoke their language, and understood their habits and style of thought, so different from ours, he fe[lt] it quite sure, if they or their tribe knew anything of the missing men, he could extract a confession from them, and by their mea[ns] is recover their bodies, for no one now doubted that they were de[ad] A plan so feasable as this met with instant approbation, and [...] he started next morning armed with a letter to the authorities to [...] t George Town, urging them to give their best assistance to [...] M'Kay, to forward the business that all were interested in. H[e] e reached George Town on Monday the 11th, and presenting his c[...] -edentials, was furnished with an order to confer with the prisoner[s] s as often as he pleased, and with another one directing the gao[...] ler to render him every assistance in his power likely to promot[e] the mission.

On entering this abode of misery he found the prisoners in a condition almost bordering on destitu[tion] ..ion, their wants most imperfectly attended to, their apartment [...] old and comfortless and themselves huddled together for a littl[e] warmth. Though the weather was icy cold, the officials with t[...] he customary apathy of the time, had allowed them no fire, th[...] next thing, after food, that a native had most difficulty to dispen[se] se with. The condition of the poor shuddering wretches made hi[m] m angry with the gaoler and they were so downcast, that it was sometime before either would speak a word in reply to his que[...] .stions. Now M'Kay is about as kind-hearted a man as you would meet with in a thousand and he could not stand the scene of w[...] -etchedness before him. His first impulse was to order a fire to b[e] e made, and everything that he thought that would be most ac[...] :ceptable to them to be provided, hot tea, bread, meat, and toba[...] cco without restriction, and to use M'Kay's homely expression, [...] *hey ate and drank like mad*, but of course gave over at last.

One of the first effects of good chee[r] ', on half famished men and women, is to produce good humou[r] '; and M'Kay noticed— after they had eaten to repletion—a very marked change in them all ; the sullen frame of mind in which he found them having quite passed off, and even the strong f[...] ceeling of aversion that they held towards the whites was a litt[le] le assuaged—at least in favour of their benefactor. The good o[...] fices of the latter pro- ceeded from a natural feeling of compa[...] ssion ; but not so " Old Sal," who having her own ends to serve, [...] had been most assiduous in her attentions to them, even though she cared not one straw

about them. She now took her place beside one of her own sex,
an extremely handsome young woman, as here and there one of
them was, named Nun… ;-in-a-bit-ta, and after a good deal of
pleasant chit-chat about matters quite foreign to the real business
she was upon, the cun… ning old faggot, by insensible degrees
brought about the subje… ct of the two missing men, and by dint
of coaxing and cajolery (after the ways of woman) wormed the
whole truth out of the p… oor simpleton, which was that they had
been killed by the men … f her own tribe. She spoke of Captain
Thomas as "Kandown… e," meaning, says M'Kay, a superior
person, such as the chie… f of an establishment which she divined
him to be, as distinguis… ied from "Rageo," which meant a common fellow, like a stoc… skeeper for example, a class of persons
whom the natives hated, Rageo being part of the term by which
they designated the De… vil, "Rageoroppa." * "When we had
got to be good friends,… says M'Kay, "she confessed that they
had died by the spears… of her tribe, and that two of the three
men then in gaol were t… he most active in the murders, which
two she declared to be M… camee and Wowee; and she volunteered
to show us the bodies of the murdered men," an offer which
M'Kay accepted directly… r, and he started for Port Sorell next
morning, accompanied by the two women, and an active constable
of the George Town poli… e, named George Warren.

The party was cros… ed over the water at Port Dalrymple
Heads, and soon reache… l Port Sorell, which they passed over,
on M'Kay signalising his … arrival on the shore opposite the landing place. He next rep… orted progress to Captain Moriarty and
Doctor Smith, informing … them at the same time that the new
arrival, Nunginabitta, kn… ew where the bodies of the murdered
men lay, but which, from … some caprice, she refused to show, if
any other except himsel… f, Warren, and Black Sal accompanied
her, and her peculiar hum… our being respected, they started under
her guidance, and she le… l them straight to where they had died.
"She took us," says Wa… rren in his evidence, "about two miles
into the bush, when they cried, and would not go… any further, but pointed to the place
where the bodies were to be found," which according to M'Kay's
statement to the jury, w… is about a hundred yards from where

---

* Robinson, in one of … his reports, gives this word as their equiva-
lent for Devil. but adds tha… t they used the same to express *thunder and
lightning*, which no doubt they connected with the Evil Presence.
M'Kay says that nearly all o… f them declared to him, in the most serious
manner, that they had seen t… he "old gentleman," at one time or another.
and were highly offended … with him if they caught him even smiling at
their credulity.

they sat down. M'Kay describes the spot where this tragedy was performed as nearly open ground, and very inferior, and as they approached the spot where Parker lay, many crows flew up from it, thus indicating the precise spot where he fell. Sixty yards further on the body of Thomas was discovered. It was thirteen days since they died, but the weather had been so cold that decomposition had not yet set in. Still the body of Parker presented a shocking spectacle, that M'Kay never speaks of, even now, without horror. I shall not perpetuate his description. Thomas seemed more like one asleep than dead.

M'Kay next went down to the port, and informed Dr. Smith he had seen the bodies, and several other persons went up under his guidance to where they were, and a kind of stage was built on which they were deposited for the night, and they were sent on to Launceston next morning, where they arrived the day afterwards.

A coroner's inquest was held directly but not concluded for several days, owing to the absence of M'Kay, who was required not only as a witness, but interpreter also. His absence was accounted for thus:—Nunginabitta had informed Old Sal (in strict confidence of course, but who blabbed directly) that her husband, Killmoronia, had taken some part in the death of Thomas, and had retreated to the Surry Hills, towards which M'Kay turned directly to pick him up, but was stopped in his advance by the first river westerly of Port Sorell, namely, the Mersey, which was then greatly swollen; and it was whilst he was making a raft to cross this dangerous stream, he learned that his new companion intended giving him the slip to rejoin her husband. But she being too important a personage to lose sight of just now, he marched her off to Launceston, where he arrived with her three or four days after the first assembling of the Coroner's jury, which both were required to attend directly. M'Kay having given his own evidence was next sworn to interpret hers. But after handing her over to the authorities she was injudiciously allowed to see the prisoners, and when she came before the jury she contradicted all she said before. It now came out she had passed the preceding night with them and she so prevaricated, that M'Kay at last told the jury " it was evident to him that a plan had been laid to get the prisoners off by contradicting her former evidence" She, however, still admitted their presence at the murders, but contended that they took no part in them. "She would not allow," says the report, "that any of the men present had anything to do with the murders, but that they were sitting down." The jury, however, did not believe her story, and all three men were adjudged to be guilty, were committed to gaol accordingly, and M'Kay bound over to appear at their trial; but the Attorney-General of the time, the shrewd but eccentric Algernon Montagu, who (if it were possible) cared less for public opinion than even the Duke of Wellington, would not prosecute, so they were discharged, that is, if consigning them to the islands of Bass' Straits could be called discharging them.

After it had become known to the men of the Big River tribe through M'Kay, that Thomas' dispositions towards their race were friendly, they expressed great sorrow at having killed him, in which M'Kay believed them to be perfectly sincere.

SEALERS *V.* BLACKS: A STRAITSMAN'S STORY.

(From notes supplied by Mr. Alexander M'Kay,)

> But on the Natives of that Land misused,
>   Not long the silence of amazement hung,
> Nor brooked they long their friendly faith abused;
>   For, with a common shriek, the general tongue
> Exclaimed, 'To arms'—and fast to arms they sprung.
> <div align="right">Sir W. Scott's <i>Vision of Don Roderick</i>.</div>

In the long contention between black and white, that followed their first rencontre at Risdon, on the 3rd of May, 1804, down to the submission of the last of the tribes to Mr. Robinson, 28th December, 1834, the worst disasters that our opponents suffered, were inflicted on them on the north-east coast of Tasmania, where (and where *only*) they had the worst of the fight.

These disasters were occasioned them by certain men of our own race, almost as savage as themselves, who occupied some of the islands of the straits, and were known in early history as the *sealers* of Banks' Straits, (that is that portion of Bass' Straits that lay between Flinders Island and the mainland, about Cape Portland). Of these men, of whom there were not thirty families or single individuals, very little intelligence has been preserved—at least in print—and of their many fights with the blacks, for the possession of their women, nothing that I know of has been communicated to the public except a few *general remarks*, written by myself, for the *Australasian* newspaper, about two years ago, which I collected from certain old M.S. documents that are preserved in the Colonial Secretary's office. But even these old papers contain few or no *details* of the many skirmishes that were fought out on the North East Coast between the sealers and the blacks, during the last 10 or 20 years of the existence of the native tribes at large, in which many lives were sacrificed on both sides. These fights ended mostly, but by no means always, to the disadvantage of the black race, who, in everything connected with bush fighting, were a very formidable foe.

The following incidents of the war, as it was carried on, on the North East Coast, are offered as illustrations of the many savage but unrecorded encounters that took place in the Cape Portland districts about 50 years ago, between the straitsmen and blacks, and may be relied on as perfectly authentic narratives:—

In about 1826, there were living on Guncarriage, now Vansittart Island, Bass' Straits, a number of sealers, that is to say several parties of them, who worked in gangs of fours or fives. Each party was furnished with a first class boat, suitable for the perilous enterprises they were so often engaged in on the rocks of the Straits, (then much resorted to by the beautiful fur-seal), often requiring them to undertake long boat voyages from group to group, during the breeding season; or to the mainlands of Australia or Tasmania as kangaroo hunters, which occupation, after the seals left our coasts, they followed as a branch of their calling.

Of these parties one was headed by a man named Duncan, who was the owner of one of these clipping boats. This person had formerly been the mate of a ship, and the crew he now worked with consisted of himself—two men who were natives of Sydney—and one other named Thomas Tucker, the last named person taking chief part in the transactions that I am about to give an account of.

Of this man Tucker, however it may have happened that he now followed the half savage life of a sealer in Bass' Straits, (a quarter then too often the refugium of men of bad character and practises,) was a gentleman by birth, education, &c, and had once held a commission in the Royal Navy; and in writing of times when Tasmania was a convict colony, it may be as well to say, that he was always a free person. A love of perilous enterprise and wild adventure, I presume it was, that threw him amongst the sealers of Bass' Straits.

He is described to me as a rather extraordinary person, of great natural talents, and acquired endowments, having had an excellent education and careful home training in youth. He was a very ingenious fellow, who could turn his hand to anything, and was therefore perfectly self-reliant, and it is believed that up to the present time his moral character was not a bad one.

He was the most daring, active and serviceable man in the Straits; and it has to be said to his credit, that he made a better use of the good training he himself had received, than almost any other person would voluntarily have done, in educating gratuitously the sealers' children, during such periods of leisure as he could snatch from his adventurous calling.

Such of the sealers, however, who had families, of whom Duncan was one, were not married to the women to whom they had united themselves. Their women were of the savage races of Australia or Tasmania, either purchased or stolen from the mainland tribes, but chiefly from those of this island, from which connexions the half-caste race now found on the islands has sprung.

Captains Kelly and Hobbs, who visited the Islands, very many years ago, and who saw a good deal of the old race of sealers, say that these poor women were mostly purchased of their parents, either for the carcasses of the seal, or for hunting dogs. But quarrels springing up between the two races, in which several of each side were killed, the natives grew chary of intercourse with the whites, and this species of barter was so much interrupted, that at last women could only be obtained by force.

Many skirmishes took place, particularly on our own coasts, for the women, the sealers making free use of their firearms, and the others spearing their opponents whenever they got a chance. The sealers had the best of the fight, and the north coast is the only part of the colony where for a while the whites really beat the blacks, many idle stories to the contrary, notwithstanding.

Captain Kelly, who was employed in 1815 and '16 on the pacific mission of making the circuit of this island, was himself nearly cut off by the blacks on several occasions. They were then very numerous, and he could scarcely ever go ashore without being attacked by them.

Having just mentioned Duncan's party at the outset, I found it necessary before proceeding to describe its movements, to say the little I have done about the principal actor of this tale, and also to describe in as few words as I could use, the cause that led to the long misunderstanding between sealer and black, I must now return to Guncarriage Island, where Duncan's people had their head quarters.

Of the four persons of whom Duncan's party consisted namely, himself, Tucker, and two young men of Sydney, the three last named were all single men, and they now sailed for the mainland of Tasmania, to secure, either by purchase or surprise, as many native girls as they wanted.

This is the first act of aggression on the liberty of the blacks, in which Tucker is known to have taken any part; but not so the others, and dearly did the natives make them pay for disturbing them in their hunting grounds.

The boat sailed accordingly for Cape Portland, carrying beside the party above named, Duncan's *wife*, as his woman was styled, and her half-caste son, an infant 2 or 3 years old. They landed on one of the beaches near Cape Portland, on land now the property of Mr. John Foster, of Hobart Town, and formed their camp under the shelter of one of the low hummocks that lie along the shore-line of this quarter

Duncan, who had been frequently engaged in feuds against the blacks, and hitherto successfully, led the fray; Tucker remaining in charge of the boat and encampment, and Duncan's son was left in his care.

The leader was a very fool-hardy fellow, and some previous successes had inspired him with such a contempt of the blacks, that it was his boast to say he was a match for any number of them. Taking his woman to act as negotiator with them, he started along with his mates in search of the Cape Portland tribe. Tucker entreated him again and again to arm his party, but could not prevail on his unreasonable mate to hear of such a thing. What, he asked, did he want with arms against mere naked black-fellows? any number of whom he could beat single-handed, whether armed or not; and accompanied as he was now by two such men as his Sydney companions, there was nothing to fear from a hundred of them, and at parting, jeeringly told his more prudent counsellor to have no fears of him, and that he would be back before night, bringing a dozen girls with him for him to choose from.

Instances of rashness like Duncan's were not uncommon on the frontier grounds of the colony during the thirty years fight between black and white. Thus Simmonds' Bay (a nook of Barnes' Bay, North Bruny) is called after a lime-burner, who sacrificed his life to a senseless feeling of contempt for the courage of the black men. This beautiful cove was great a place of great resort of the Bruny tribe, and their intrusions, as Simmonds thought them, were resented by him, as though *they*, and not *he*, were the trespassers on the ground he occupied, and they were ordered off whenever they came. Mistaking his commands for requests, they were at first complied with. But finding them so frequently repeated, they got tired of them at last. On these occasions, it was his custom to take a stick with him to beat them off if necessary. The last notice that Simmonds gave them to quit was late in November of 1822; but they began to understand him by this time, and laughed in his face for his impertinence, whereon he struck the one nearest him. But this was the last act of his life, for the offended black turned on him like a tiger, drove his spear through him, and he was a dead man the next moment.

Duncan's woman soon got traces of the tribe they were in pursuit of, and came on their huts it is believed in the afternoon, or even earlier. The Cape Portland natives hated the sealers, and none more so than Duncan himself, whom they recognised immediately. Snatching down their spears from the trees in which they customarily stuck them when in repose, they only waited till he was within range ; then, with the fatal aim for which they were so famous, he was struck in nearly all parts of his body at once. He fell of course, death ensuing instantaneously.

The two Sydney men fled for their lives directly ; and as the blacks did not pursue them at once, they succeeded in gaining the coast, but at a considerable distance from the camp before they were overtaken. They plodded on rapidly towards the boat but failed to reach it, the superior agility of the blacks proving too much for them. The particulars of the meeting have been too imperfectly preserved for narration, but as their dead bodies were found a few days afterwards in a shockingly mutilated state, no doubt was left about who were the authors of this massacre.

Duncan's woman remained with her own race. Glad of regaining her liberty, she voluntarily rejoined them ; and without regret, resigned to chance the half-caste offspring of her forced connection with Duncan.

It is a remarkable fact, but vouched for by Mr. G. A. Robinson, that the black women though passionately fond of children of their own blood, as a rule detested such as they bore to white men ; and on this occasion Duncan's woman abandoned her only son with perfect unconcern.

In following the relation that I have received of these transactions, the narrative reconducts me to the sealers camp at Cape Portland.

The first and second day of Tucker's solitude closed, but Duncan and his companions returned not to the boat ; and he grew more and more uneasy as their absence was prolonged, till a sentiment of fear for their safety overpowered every other feeling. It was in vain that he endeavoured to suppress the idea that some evil had befallen them, the presentiment that was on him grew the stronger the more he strove to dismiss it from his mind. He tried to believe it possible that they had failed to reach the tribe so soon as they hoped, and were still in pursuit ; but this hope vanished as he remembered they had made no provision for an absence of more than a few hours, after which they should have returned. they might have lost themselves—but this was most unlikely in a nearly open district, and with a native woman for a guide, who could have retraced their steps one by one to the boat, like a bloodhound ; and his belief settled at last into an immutabe conviction that they would not come back again. Frequently during the second day, did he fire off his piece to notify the position of the camp in case they might be returning, but the precaution was an useless one, and its echoes were its sole response. He passed the night in restless anxiety and was abroad at day dawning of the third morning, watching on the sandhill, but to no purpose. He returned to his tent sick at heart and lay down, whilst Duncan's little child amused itself outside as he best could. Young as this infant was, he had even now a little of the cunning and vigilance of the race he belonged to, by the mother's side at least, and Tucker, though half wearied out, noticed that he kept running in and out of the tent, with unusual frequency, and an evident desire to communicate something he was too young to explain. But the sealer unhappily gave less heed than he ought to the peculiar movements of the child, and he remained within.

But at this instant he was effectually aroused from his inaction by a volley of spears and stones striking the tent with uncommon force, accompanied by the shouts of the natives who were now surrounding his domicile. Tucker sprung to his feet, and seizing his two-barrel gun and the child, he got to the top of the sandhill mentioned above, before a second spear was thrown, determined if die he must, there to defend himself as he best could to the last. He had plenty ammunition and was a deadly shot, which latter fact was known to the tribe, but more particularly to at least two of the most forward of those savages, who had been on the Straits islands along with him before this time. Directily he was gone from the tent, the natives took possession of it and of his boat also, which latter they tried to set fire to, but from some unexplained cause, they failed to damage it much.

Amongst the natives present, he observed Duncan's woman, and the two men spoken of just above, to whom he was known. These young fellows had been taken in infancy, and were brought up amongst our own people, by whom they were named respectively Murray and Jack. Both of them had lived much in Hobart Town, where they earned a living on the water, either as boatmen or sailors, and both had visited the Straits islands in the sealing season, in vessels fitted out for the seal trade, and more than once had worked the seal rookeries in company with Tucker. But as usual with these *civilised blacks*, as they were called, their natural hankerings for savage life never departed from them, and they were as difficult to tame permanently as wolves or wood pigeons are, unless when taken so young as to retain no remembrance of the wild life to which they were born; and there is hardly an instance of their not rejoining their own people on reaching manhood, and it was observed of these particular individuals that they were ever afterwards the most forward and mischevious of the tribe, and the directors of their movements in their numerous hostile incursions into the settled districts; and now, by Tucker's own account, these two young men, more than any of the rest, evinced the most determined hostility towards him, "and did all they could," says the account I am writing from, "to get at and kill him." But the well directed piece of this unerring marksman, as they well knew him to be, kept them back. Luckily the great body of them were more intent on plundering his tent and boat, than on murder, or his life was not worth a minute's purchase, for though he might have killed or disabled two or three of them in an united onslaught, they were far too numerous to be kept long at bay in any general attack. Tucker now called out to Duncan's woman to come to him, promising not to fire, if she came alone, and she did so. He then enquired what had become of his companions; but it was long before he could get at the facts, for she was either afraid or disinclined to speak out, and she prevaricated and fenced every question, like an unwilling witness under legal examination. They had gone, she first at pretended, to Launceston, then somewhere else, or were away with some of the tribe hunting, and would soon be back, "but all of which," says M'Kay'a manuscript, "he knew to be wrong." Tucker was a patient fellow, but her evasions wore out even his patience in time, and so annoyed him, that he pointed his piece at her at last, saying unless she let him know what had happened them, he would blow her head off where she stood, when she owned that the natives had killed them all—Duncan certainly, and the others she believed. He next asked her whether she would return to the islands with him, or remain with her tribe? She chose to stay where she was.

The day wore on, and Tucker still kept his post on the top of the sand-cone, no one caring to take his first shots. Indeed most of them seemed satisfied with the mischief they had already done, and some of them left with their shares of the plunder of his tent. He observed their indifference, and through Duncan's woman entered into a parley with them, proposing that they should give him his boat and let him go, promising not to fire on any one if this were done; and as night was coming on, and they themselves wished to get back to their camp, his proposal was agreed to, and some women were sent to assist him in launching the boat, which was put into the water, and Tucker went down to the beach to embark, Duncan's boy following closely behind him. But just as he was going to step into her, a native man who was crouching within some boobialla scrub, sprung from his hiding place, and snatching up the child, ran off with it to some rocks, and then giving it a swing over his head, dashed its brains out against them. The sealer instinctively raised his piece for a shot at the murderer, but remembering his promise not to fire on anyone, and that his own safety depended on his keeping his word, the man escaped for the present. But Tucker marked him. It was Murray.

The wind blew off the land when he commenced his dreary night's voyage homewards, and he steered for the islands under a mizen only, the boat's mainsail and jib, of which his tent was made, being left with the natives. The breeze, however, was fresh and fair, and he kept before it all night, and when morning broke was off Preservation Island, on which he soon afterwards landed.

From this time forward Tucker's whole nature seemed changed. He was perhaps never a good man, but he was not a cruel one. But the loss of his mates, and the dangers he had so lately escaped from, gave rapid expansion to whatever evil there was within him, the latent seeds of which, like the prophets gourd, grew into maturity in a single night, but unlike it withered not away again. He was, moreover, as we have seen, fond of children, and the horrid death of one he had charge of only yesterday, gave intensity to a passion for revenge which now began to dominate over his reason.

Several other sealers to whom he was known were staying on Preservation Island, and to them he told the disastrous story of the death of his mates, and easily engaged them to assist in avenging it; and so as soon as the wind served, they sailed for Cape Portland, well armed and equipped for a murderous fight with the blackfellows.

Cape Portland is more properly a point of land than a cape. The shore hereabouts is almost everywhere low, and presents many points where a landing may be made in moderate weather. The country about it is not a fertile one, the best of it that I now remember, are a few hundred acres, in the midst of which it is that the pleasant homestead of Mr. John Foster, of Hobart Town, is planted. It was not far from here that the sealers landed, forming a temporary camp of their sails. But the wandering tribe had left the neighbourhood for other hunting grounds by this time, and their search after them, though it broke best part of a week, was an unavailing one, and they returned to the islands.

But Tucker never afterwards relinquished the idea of taking a full revenge on the Cape Portland tribe, wherever he might fall in with it; and above all, to destroy, if possible, the two youths, Jack and Murray. He made no secret of his intentions, and all the sealing community knew them; and as the sympathies of the large majority of these half lawless men were with Tucker, they quite approved his determination.

There was, however, one party of them who took no part in the many contentions that occurred at this time, now 1827, between sealer and black, but who managed to keep on good terms with the latter throughout, and there was perfect confidence between them and the tribes of the north-east coast of the colony. The leader of this party, as he was styled, from being the owner of their boat, was named Thompson. The natives knew his boat and never retreated when they saw it approaching the mainland, or took any precaution if they found that he was in her. All the sealers resorted to the mainland at times to take kangaroos, the skins of which have been in demand in this market, time out of mind. But Thompson's crew was the only one with whom the natives now held friendly intercourse, and when they met, many kind offices were done on both sides. Did Thompson's people want help to beach or unbeach their boat, the blacks were ready to lend a hand, or they would bring wood or water to his camp; whilst he on his part would cross them to the off-lying rocks during the egging season, and recross them to the main afterwards; give them seal carcasses, &c., &c.

It is said by Robinson in one of his many reports on the condition of the blacks (January 24th, 1831), that none of the natives of the North or East Coasts had the least idea of making or using a catamaran, like those dwelling on the South and West Coast districts had. Indeed, the configuration of the shores he is speaking of, which are not much broken into bays, gave them little occasion to trust themselves afloat; and as no Tasmanian native ever gave himself the smallest unnecessary trouble, these "machines," as Robinson calls them, were never constructed by them; so if the North or East Coast tribes desired to visit any of the bird rocks that were not within swimming distance, they had no means of doing so unless a friendly boatman were at hand, to cross and recross them. Thompson, when he had leisure, never refused them this service, thus enabling them in egging time to add largely to their food supplies.

The tribes who formerly roamed about Cape Portland had now no other white associates excepting Thompson and his crew; and he took advantage of a visit from the horde, whom Tucker and others had lately tried to surprise, to put them on their guard against the designs of this man, and more particularly told them of the certain doom of Murray and Jack, if they gave him the chance of a shot at them.

The sealing season of 1827 was approaching; and of the

boats that took part in it, one was from Hobart Town. On its passage to the straits, the crew put in for one night at the Eddystone boat harbour, at a moment when the Cape Portland tribe were hunting there. The boat's crew, as too usual with sailors, were a careless set of fellows, and not thinking in the least of danger, kept no lookout for squalls of any kind when ashore; and after forming a rude shelter for the night, retired within to refresh, a good while before dusk, leaving their boat at anchor, but with the stern-fast ashore. The men of the Cape Portland tribe were just the reverse of our sailors, that is, they were ever on the watch, either to do mischief to others or avoid danger, and had no difficulty in surprising the strangers, who, all at once, found their place of refuge encircled by a cordon of armed savages. Our sailors fired a random shot or two, and then ran to their boat, amidst such a whizzing of spears, as they had not dreamed of hearing when they landed. Luckily for them it had grown pretty dark by this time, and the usually fine aim of the black was not very true. The crew reached the boat and got off, but some of them were very badly wounded.

Many boats and scores of homesteads were thus surprised every year by "the poor benighted down-trodden savages," as it was the fasion of silly despatch-writers and sentimental pamphleteers to style this clever but sanguinary race of men, who were the aggressors in nearly every skirmish, who for many years kept the colony in a greater state of alarm than the bushrangers did, and whose final extinction was far more due to a combination of disastrous natural causes converging simultaneously on their camps, than to the bullet of the white settler, or even the extraordinary daring and judgment of Mr. Robinson.

After the above described specimen of native subtlety, the Hobart Town sealing party stuck to their boat till they reached the straits islands, not again touching the mainland during their voyage. They skirted along the north eastern shore of Cape Barren Island, and eventually landed on Guncarriage, where Tucker had his home, and where he unhappily was then to receive them.

He was never slow or chary of giving his assistance to any one visiting his island home, more especially to men in distress like these new arrivals were; and he now collected a few other fellows to help them unload their boat and beach her, which done, he conducted them to his neat little cottage, that stood near the landing place.

"What's up with you?" was his first enquiry after they were settled down in his cottage, "What's the matter. Some o' ou seem badly hurt."

"The natives—the natives at Eddystone harbor," said one of the wounded men.

"Those damned Cape Portlanders, I warrant it," said Tucker with emphasis, "the most bloody tribe on the coast. They hunt there and as far south as George's Bay. It's only the other day like, that they killed three of my own mates, and a boy belonging to one of them ; and now it's not their fault, but your good luck, that they have not killed all of you. But we will talk over the affair after I have stopped the shotholes they have put through you, for I am surgeon and everything at these islands."

He found that two of the five were badly hit, and one other more slightly. The two former he thought would not be able to do much during the approaching season ; however he was quite surgeon enough to deal with worse cases than these ; he dressed their wounds, and otherwise treated them so professionally, that in about eight weeks the two worst of them were able to resume light work.

About a week after landing at Guncarriage, the sealing work began ; and Tucker who often worked the rocks on the East Coast, and was still hankering for a brush with the blacks, resolved to commence operations where he would be within reach of the tribe if they came down to the coast during the time he was there. Of the unwounded strangers who joined him for the season, one was—Rogers, and the others Little and Sydney. These three and a native woman called Dumpy, with whom Tucker was now allied, completed the party.

Tucker said nothing to his new friends about his designs on the natives ; nor had they any suspicion of them through extra preparations being made for the trip in the shape of guns and ammunition ; for as sealing was mostly carried on by shooting from the boat, these articles were necessarily supplied in abundance for their legitimate work.

So soon as the wind served they started for the East Coast, and first worked the George rock, about five miles northerly of Eddystone Point. Here they remained about a couple of nights, and then left for the sealers' refuge, as they called the little boat harbour at Eddystone Point. At this refuge the sealers had a permanent camp consisting of two good huts, that were used in common by the straitsmen as their occasions required, when they were kangaroo hunting on shore. Here they landed with such things as they required. They breakfasted, and then Rogers, Little, and Sydney, who were very tired, went into the hut to rest, leaving Tucker and the woman outside at the fire, and were soon asleep.

The Cape Portland tribe were still here, though not close to the harbour at this moment. But as day advanced some indications of their approach, which no European would observe, reached the ears of the black woman; but she said nothing until better assured of the fact. Tucker and her still sat by the fire, smoking their pipes, while their mates slept. The land all along the north-eastern shores is very open, so that with the commonest vigilance there was no danger of any sudden surprise. All at once, however, the woman started and whispered to Tucker, "here are the blackfellows," pointing at them at the same time. He looked round just in time to see the head of one of them peering at them over a low rise, which was withdrawn directly, and not a vestige of the hundreds who were creeping stealthily on them, to surround them, was to be seen. Our natives managed their attacking movements with uncommon skill, and hundreds are the instances of their sorrounding dwellings in perfect swarms without their exciting the smallest suspicion of their being at hand. No more subtle a race could be than the Tasmanian savages.

Tucker was not an easily alarmed man at any time, and was not much intimidated even now. His double gun, which was loaded and ready for instant work, lay near at hand, and as his mates had their sealing rifles, they were not to be trifled with when they were on the look-out. Knowing that the blacks never fought at disadvantage, he judged there would be no immediate attack. He therefore called out to them, through the woman, to let them know that he saw them, and was ready for them if they meant fighting, but, if not, that he did not wish to hurt them. His tone was friendly, but his words were those of deceit. Several heads were now seen since they discovered that they were observed, on which he invited two or three of them to come over to him, all the rest to keep back. But they hesitated, none relishing an interview with a man whom they had robbed and tried to kill so very lately, and it was long before he could soothe them into a good humour.

"What are you afraid of?" said he, "Come over, but not too many of you; we shan't hurt you. Is Murray with you? Let him and Jack and two or three others come, but not more, and I will give them as much tobacco and other things for all hands as they choose to carry away."

Jack and Murray were there, but still held back.

"We not come," said both the youths together (for they spoke the language very fairly). "Thompson tell us you shoot us."

"Then Thompson's a liar," said he, "I would sooner shoot him than you. I never told him so. Not I. I could have shot you, Murray, if I had chosen, when you killed the child, but I let you go, and will not hurt you now, so either come over to us, or *all* of you go away."

His promises of friendship and the presents he would give them, at length reassured them, and four of them came, namely, a young man named Limaganna, a youth of about fourteen, (whom M'Kay says was the handsomest native he ever saw,) besides Jack and Murray. Others would have come, but Tucker motioned them to keep off, the woman telling them he would have no more of them, and cautioned them all to come no nearer, otherwise they would take to their boat.

Tucker then set them down to breakfast, and whilst they were busy with the good things before them, he rose up quite unconcernedly and went to the hut where Rogers, Little, and Sydney were still sleeping heavily after their recent fatigue, and the discomforts of the George's rocks, for neither of them were so hardy as Tucker. He woke them quietly, telling them to get up directly and bring out their rifles, as the natives were all around them.

Rogers and the others had had quite enough of the natives when at Eddystone Harbour some days ago, to last them for the rest of their lives and the intelligence that they had got into a second scrape with them in a fortnight was disheartening. Suddenly aroused from their heavy sleep, they scarcely knew what they were doing at first, for they were half stupefied, by being thus hastily awoke. Up to this time neither of them knew anything of Tucker's evil designs on the men whom they saw sitting at their fire, to which he had entrapped them; but thinking of nothing but their own safety, they did as they were bid and followed him.

The fifth and last act of the tragedy, I will give as nearly as I can in M'Kay's own words:—

" Sydney has told me many a time. 'I took up my gun as we all did, not knowing what was the matter. When we came out, there were the natives at breakfast. Murray sitting on a water keg, and the rest on the ground. I saw poor Murray's heart beat again as we approached, guns in hand, to where he sat. His pannican full of tea dropped to the ground as we came near, and he saw Tucker cocking his rifle. In two two steps Tucker was beside him, and said to him, " Murray, you have lived long enough," drew the triggers of his double-barrel, and both charges went into his heart. He fell dead directly. The other natives jump up, and Limaganna ran off, Rogers who was yet hardly awake, presented at Limaganna, when Tucker calls out (pointing to Jack), "Jacky's your mark—Jacky's your mark." Poor Jack called out "No, no," that is imploring him not to shoot him, and holding both hands before his face retreated hastily backwards. Rogers fired but missed him, when he turned quickly round, and ran rapidly down to the sea. Sydney neither fired nor meant to fire, for by this time he began to think there was something not right. But Tucker's thirst for blood was not yet slaked, and noticing Sydney's hesitation, and that Jack was escaping, snatched the rifle from his hand Taking his usual steady aim at his victim, the bullet passed into the back of his head, and he ran no further.

"Limaganna escaped, but the boy clung to the woman, and implored her not to let him be killed. Tucker, whose vengance was now appeased, looked at him mildly, and by kind words and some presents calmed his fears, and allowed him to rejoin his people, who were withdrawing, and the sealing party left to re-commence work.

"Sydney was very angry with Tucker for what he had done, and has often told me he was very sorry ever after that he was accidentally present at these murders, even though he took no part in them.

"Limagarna, and also a brother of his, were both shot in some farm fight at Break o'Day Plains, in 1830; and the next year, the boy now about 15 years of age, was made prisoner by me along with some other natives of Musselrow River, and was sent to the aboriginal establishment in the Straits.

Mr. Alexander M'Kay, from whom I received the outline sketch of the above narrative, is now a settler at Peppermint Bay, D'Entrecasteux Channel, where he has resided more than 30 years. He is about 68 years old, but hale and strong in an uncommon degree, the natural consequence of a life of activity, and a constitution that has never been abused by unhealthy indulgences. I have known him well for about three and forty years. We are very old bush chums, and have walked some thousands of miles together; and I can say truly of him that he is the best bush companion I have ever had. Full of anecdote, no one knows more of the old times than he, and as no one has ranged the colony more than M'Kay, (between 1825 and '40) his local knowledge is extensive. He was in early life one of the first employes of the Van Diemen's Land Company, as explorer at one time, and master of one of their crafts at another, for he was a sailor by profession. From the service of the company he passed into that of the Aboriginal Mission under Robinson, to whom he rendered important services, But [conceiving himself to ¿be neglected by his chief, he threw up his engagement.

Quitting Guncarriage Island, where the captive natives were domiciled before their removal to the establishment which they called Wyba Luma, on Flinders Island, he proceeded to Hobart Town, and Colonel Arthur, who had a very high opinion of him. immediately gave him a command independent of Mr. Robinson, in which he soon distinguished himself.

Before quitting Robinson, M'Kay had been twenty-three weeks on Guncarriage by himself, in charge of a large body of recently captured blacks, all as wild as wolves; and it is amongst the chief marvels of his adventurous and really extraordinary career, that he escaped with his life from amongst them.

THE EARLY YEARS

OF THE

LAST OF THE TASMANIANS.

"All perished—I alone am left on earth
To whom nor relative nor blood remains,
No—not a kindred drop that runs in human veins."

CAMPBELL's *Gertrude of Wyoming*.

The following is M'Kay's account of some passages in the life of this woman—the last of her race—as communicated to him by herself :—

"On the 16th or thereabouts, of January, 1830, I first saw Truganini, we took her, also her husband, and two of his boys by a former wife, and two other women, the remains of the tribe of Bruny Island, when I went with Mr. Robinson round the island. I think she was about 18 years of age, her father was chief of Bruny Island, name Mangana. She had an uncle, I don't know his native name, the white people called him Boomer, he was shot by a soldier. I will now give you some of her own account of what she knew :—We were camped close to Partridge Island when I was a little girl, when a vessel came to anchor without our knowledge of it, a boat came on shore, and some of the men attacked our camp. We all ran away, but one of them caught my mother, and stabbed her with a knife, and killed her My father grieved much about her death, and used to make a fire at night by himself, when my mother would come to him. I had a sister named Moorina ; she was taken away by a sealing boat. I used to go to Birch's Bay ; there was a party of men cutting timber for the Government there, the overseer was Mr. Munro ; while I was there two young men of my tribe came for me, one of them was to have been my husband, his name was Paraweena. Well, two of the sawyers said they would take us in a boat to

Bruny Island, which we agreed to. When we got about half-way across the Channel, they murdered the two natives, and threw them overboard, but one of them held me. Their names were Watkin Lowe and Paddy Newell, this was the account she gave me many times."

For the use of those who may not be well acquainted with the places named in the previous note ; or whose recollections may not extend back very far, I beg to supply a few particulars :— At the time when M'Kay became acquainted with the woman he writes about, the Bruny Island tribe was reduced to six persons. It was formerly a very numerous one, and only six months before was probably eight or ten times as strong as in January of 1830. Disease, which had been thining our natives for years past, was peculiarly fatal at the time M'Kay writes of and afterwards. According to one of Robinson's reports, dated 23rd of September, 1829, no fewer than twenty-two of this tribe had died in the preceding fifteen weeks, or about three a fortnight ; but of those who went off between September and January there is no report.

To most readers residing in the South, I presume it will be known that Partridge Island is in D'Entrecasteaux Channel, very close to one of the points of South Bruny, and about forty miles from Hobart Town. It was so named by Admiral Bruny D'Entrecasteaux. When I first knew it, 1830, it was generally called Santo's Island, why, I know not. It has now recovered its proper name. Birch's Bay is also in this Channel, where there was formerly a large Government sawing establishment. The *overseer*, as Truganini styles Mr. Peter Munro, who was the superintendent of the establishment, a designation, which in the Governmental service meant something very much above an overseer. I knew him well and a most excellent and gentlemanly person he was.

M'Kay, who writes but seldom—like most to whom writing is troublesome—is less communicative with his pen than his tongue. I shall therefore supply anything that he has omitted from his note, from his conversations with me about the savage butchery of these striplings ; to which I shall add what I knew of the vagabond Lowe, who I will venture to say, was the originator of these murders.

When these men had conveyed the two youths and the girl about half way across the Channel, which may be a mile and a half wide hereabouts, the horrible tragedy commenced by the two boatmen throwing both the young fellows into the water. Directly they were overboard and the girl secured, they took to to their oars, and using all their strength, they pulled away from them, leaving them either to drown or to regain the land if they could. But the young blacks were both fast swimmers, and overhauled the boat before she had much way on her, and laying hold of the gunwales tried to get in again; but this was most effectually prevented by one of the boatmen seizing a hatchet and chopping off their hands near the wrist, in which disabled state the poor creatures went down, and the murderers got clear off with their prize—the poor girl—who had just witnessed the shocking massacre of her young companions.

But as legal punishment never overtook a white man for the murder of an aboriginal, so these homicides escaped; neglect, or a combination of lucky circumstances, always interposed to prevent enquiry. The girl could not *then* speak a word of English, and as the murderers kept silence nothing was ever known of this infernal transaction, until she first revealed it to M'Kay, but not until the men had escaped, and could not be brought to trial, if that would have availed anything at the time.

Newell must have been as depraved a felon as Lowe, but as I knew something of the latter, and not of the other, I can only speak decisively of Lowe. He was one of those fellows having no higher aspirations than to be thought a clever scoundrel, and he gloried in the reputation which his evil deeds had acquired for him. He was a perfect master of villany in whatever shape it was to be achieved, and the practice of knavery was the business of his life.

It is now more than forty years since I knew him, loafing about a district with not a dozen persons in it, and where it might have been thought there was little opening for the exercise of such talents as his. But he found a way to employ them, and carried desolation to one hearth. His final act in the colony, after becoming free, was quite of a piece with all his antecedent practices.

At the time I am speaking of, Hobart Town was as much defiled by the presence of a low class of usurers as the holy temple itself eighteen or nineteen centuries before. No risk was too great for these worthies. Money was often obtainable on the most questionable security, but at such an enormous rate of interest as must have contemplated an occasional default.

Lowe, who had been in every gaol and chain gang of the colony, was heartily sick of Tasmania by the time his original and cumulative sentences had expired, and he longed to return home. But as he had not a shilling some device had to be hit on, whereby money enough could be raised to pay his passage, and which a fellow so gifted as he, was not slow to discover.

Clever and keen as money lenders are reputed to be, it struck Lowe that there must be some way of doing them, and a bright idea flashed upon him, "all of a moment," as he afterwards expressed it, that eventually enabled him to pluck one of them quite to his mind.

To this end he either wrote a letter, or got some convict law clerk to do it for him, addressed to himself, purporting to be written by the executors of a lately deceased person. This letter, after acquainting him that a rich uncle of his had given up the ghost, proceeded to congratulate the fortunate Mr. Lowe on his accession to a considerable fortune, and concluded by advising either his immediate return to England with the necessary credentials of identity, or to forward a power of attorney to some friend to act for him, &c., &c. The letter was entrusted to a seaman in the plot who was returning to England, by whom it was posted in London, and in due time it reached the hands of the quondam convict, and incredible as it may appear to us now, he actually found someone to advance a good sum on the faith of this letter of advice, and Lowe having given the necessary acknowledgement of indebtedness, took ship to England, and has never been heard of from that day to this.

Since the foregoing narrative of the early history of the woman Truganini—the very last of the aboriginal people of Tasmania—went to the press, she too has "gone to her long home," having died on Tuesday the 8th of May, 1876, at the age of about sixty-four.

As it will be found in another part of this history of the extermination of the blacks, she was one of those whom Mr Robinson employed to induce them to surrender, and whom he never could have subdued but for her and a few others of her race. To him it undoubtedly is that the merit belongs of devising and executing the plans that led to their removal from the mainland of Tasmania; but to others, and chiefly Truganini, was entrusted the perilous duty of negotiating with the tribes to lay down their arms, and submit themselves to the paternal custody, such as it proved to be, of a Government happily long since extinct.

I hope there are none amongst the readers of this narrative who have not perceived, that in the performance of the task thus assigned her, she was powerless to evade it. Acting under the guidance of a man who, astute as he naturally was, was himself greviously deceived by false representations of the ulterior designs of the Government on the liberties of this people, which were doubtlessly communicated to his employees, she followed his leading almost necessarily. To this it has to be added, that he had acquired an ascendancy so complete over those of these simple minded savages whom he had subdued to his service, as to have left them almost literally without the faculty of volition. Hence he often urged them on enterprises of danger that they would have willingly evaded, had it been permitted them to consult their own inclinations. In several of his official reports, he acknowledges engaging them in embassies so fraught with peril, that death seemed the certain consequence of their obedience. All his interviews with the still unsubdued tribes, were preceded by negotiations first opened by his "friendly natives," as he calls these humble agents, in which Truganini took so prominent a part, that it is said when the deluded blacks found themselves prisoners, they often taunted her with being the author of their downfall. (See *Tasmanian Tribune*, 9th of May, 1876). But the poor woman could have had no idea of the doom that awaited them.

To other services this community, and prominently Robinson himself, owed this last survivor of a now wholly extinct nation, was his own preservation from death in the midst of his useful career; when she displayed such courage as was creditable to her in a very high degree. The details of this adventure, where these two, after a savage assault on the lives of their party by a horde of infuriated blacks, were separated from the others and driven into the Arthur River, where but for her he must have perished, are given in a former page. In his official reports of this repulse, he does not indicate the woman who preserved him; but in his private conversations he always named her as the one to whom he owed his escape. Of those to whom he related it some are still in life.

The age of Truganini has been recently computed to be seventy-three; but this is a mistake for she was not nearly so old. At the time of her capture, 16th of January, 1830, she was only about eighteen, which fixes he birth, approximately, at 1812. Her age was therefore but little over sixty-four. Her birth, it may be presumed, happened when Colonel Andrew Geils administered the Government of Tasmania.

Throughout this history, wherever her name occurs, I have adopted the orthography of Robinson, namely, *Truganini*. But I have lately been informed by Mr. J. W. Graves, who has paid particular attention to her own pronunciation of it, that it should be spelled *Trucanini*, which is the term by which her tribe designated a plant found by the sea side, which we call *barilla*.

NARRATIVE OF A TRIP TO OYSTER COVE IN 1855.

The following narrative of a journey I made in April, 1855, from Hobart Town to Oyster Cove, and published at the time in a local newspaper, long since defunct, embodies much information of the condition of these people as I then saw them ; and if I have slightly altered it from the form in which it originally appeared, it has been to incorporate it with this account of our native tribes :—

Circumstances, the relation of which would in no way interest the reader, required me to make the journey from Kingston (10 miles south of Hobart Town) to the neighbourhood of Oyster Cove, the dwelling place of the few remaining aboriginal people of Tasmania, which is distant, overland from Hobart Town, about 23 miles. Desirous of preserving some memorial of this excursion, I made a few notes as I went along, from which, in an after leisure hour, I have compiled the following narrative for the perusal of such as may take an interest in the subjects it treats of.

The village of Kingston is an irregular straggling country township, a mere assemblage of scattered cottages, situate near to a small stream called Brown's River—a small rill. Several of these buildings are mere huts, but others are good brick residences ; the entire number being about a dozen.

The morning of my departure was one of sunshine ; and I started with a young companion, who travelled, like myself, a-foot, fresh for the journey, and in such spirits for a walk as fine weather usually produces. We took the principal highway, of course, but from which only a very imperfect knowledge of the district it traverses is to be acquired, as it is generally directed across a barren waste ; and the traveller judging of the country from road-side experiences only would form a very erroneous opinion of the District. With the exception of that part where it crosses the fine estate belonging to Mr. Baynton, he sees little but barren sands, stunted trees, and a herbage indicative of sterility and worthlessness. But this would be an unfair description of this district, which is called Kingborough, where some excellent farms are to be found, the best soils of which are very little inferior to those of Pittwater. Mr. Baynton's farm is very prolific, and his house and homestead are excellent though, in strict accordance with the prevailing tastes of Tasmanian farmers, every tree that once stood near it has been carefully rooted out, thus imparting an air of nake'ness to the place which is most displeasing. Farmers, like others, must consult their own tastes and not those of passers-by, but it has often surprised me to see the indifference with which they throw down all the indigenous forest trees in the neighbourhood of their dwellings, many of which are often exquisitely handsome, and after destroying in a few weeks what a century could not replace, they then often commence planting. But it is not the reproach of Mr. Baynton to have done anything to give shelter to his substantial farm-house, or to beautify its neighbourhood.

A short walk from hence and we reach the shores of North West Bay, along which the road leads for a little distance. This is a large arm of the sea, but, being shut in on all sides by unpicturesque hills, it is not a pleasing place. Approaching North West Bay River, the soil sensibly improves in character, and the coarse grey sands we have passed over are succeeded by a rich red soil of great fertility. The farms hereabouts are small and strictly agricultural, the breeding of stock not being attended to. At this place the stream flows through a rich alluvium, second to nothing in Tasmania.

The floods of last year (1854), having demolished the bridge that used to span this stream (a Government structure and therenot meant to last), we floundered through it with luckily no more damage than a few contusions, the usual penalty of fording a Tasmanian river, and halted at a road-side inn called the "Half-way House," (half-way to where I was not so fortunate as to discover, as all beyond it is a wilderness of forests). It is kept by a person named Groombridge, whose studious civilities made some slight amends for his rough exterior; and, that our brief stay at his house might be as pleasant as possible, he obliged us with his company at breakfast, and gratified us with the details of many local and domestic matters that no one cared anything about but himself. Still had it not been for rather an unpleasant practice he had of now and then blowing his nose in the corner of the tablecloth, he would have passed for a very nice fellow. Near the Half-way House are several cottages, possibly the nucleus of a future town. Two or three of these already assume the name, if not the reality, of "general stores," but judging from the wares exhibited in the windows, which are limited to a few boxes of lucifers, pipes, and a very small unostentatious display of lollipops, it struck even such unobserving travellers as ourselves that the designation, like the name of the hamlet itself, Margate, had been prematurely assumed.

We resumed our walk. For several miles the road passes a very uninteresting tract of country. The soil is a miserable white loam, producing only stringy-bark trees, derisively called "bull's wool" by bushmen, from the peculiar texture of the bark. They were much scorched by bush fires. At two miles from Margate we crossed a small stream called the Snug River, which discharges its waters into a little inlet, that is so secluded as to have acquired this name. At a short distance from hence are the remains of a once excellent edifice, built originally by the district magistrate, which the destructive bush fires of January, 1854, destroyed, the brick walls excepted. It was then an inn; and at an outhouse, which has since been made habitable, the business has been re-commenced. The landlord, Mr. Haines, had a lamentable tale of misfortune to tell us; but the burning of his premises and furniture was hardly so distressing as his account of the misconduct of the vagabond sawyers and splitters of the neighbourhood, who, under pretence of giving assistance, robbed him of everything they could rescue from the fire.

The last four or five miles of the journey, to Oyster Cove we found the road passing over a succession of high and pretty steep hills, from some points of which we caught an occasional view of a very beautiful landscape; though, from the frequent intervention of trees, it was not seen to the greatest advantage. Now and then only, where an opening occurred, could we get a fair view of it; but, at th every few points where trees were few, we greatly admired the varied and magnificent picture that lay before us. The dusky eminences of South Bruny, stretched along the horizon, terminating in the south east in the bold and beautiful cliffs of the Fluted Cape. Adventure Bay, on the east of Bruny—the place of anchorage of the famous old navigators Cook, Furneaux, and Bligh, last century—lies fully in view, separated from the nearer waters of D'Entrecasteaux Channel by the long, low, thread-like isthmus that unites the two peninsulas of Bruny Island. This singular strip of sand looks more like an artificial embankment, as seen from a distance, than a natural barrier raised to resist the heavy ocean swell of the Pacific. Within the visible horizon of these open spaces, is contained nearly all of Bruny (32 miles long) with its deep and many inlets, and a vast extent of undulating country in the east and north east, fronting on the most varied coast line in the world, forming altogether a picture which well repays the toil of a long journey to see it.

But let us push forward, and soon a bend in the ever-winding road places the traveller in full view of the establishment at which the few remaining descendants of the first inhabitants of Tasmania are located. At this point, though the road has been gradually falling off for a mile or more, the traveller still finds himself at an elevation much above the level of the glen assigned them for their abiding place for the last few years of their still unexpired existence. Occupying now comparatively low ground, the landscape, though still eminently beautiful, is greatly reduced in extent, and most of the scene faintly described above is now shut out by nearer hills that we before stood above and looked over. But if the view were a hundred times more prepossessing than it is, its attractions would be scarcely observed at an instant that places before us an object, which, though mean and unimposing, is, on account of its inmates, the only thing the stranger traveller can look at.

Standing in view of this dreary edifice, rude though it is, and in vile contrast with the landscape around, both the eye and mind seem actually to refuse to rest on any other object. How, indeed, should it be otherwise, when we know that within the walls of that desolate-looking shealing are all who now remain of a once formidable people, whom a "thirty years war" with our own countrymen have swept into captivity, and their relatives to the grave; a war which, notwithstanding our ultimate success, we derived little credit from.

The glen in which they vegetate, rather than live, derives its name from the little inlet in front of it, Oyster Cove, a small arm of D'Entrecasteaux Channel, so abounding in mud-flats that a row-boat cannot reach the shore, except at high-tide. Between the beach and the building they occupy is a small salt marsh, but as the ground rises a little it improves in character, changing into a fertile alluvium, but of very limited extent, five or six acres only, all behind it being more barren, if possible, than the sand of the sea shore, producing nothing but useless herbage and forest trees dwarfed into mere bushes by the exceeding infertility of the land.

The building they inhabit a part of, is a long low narrow range formed of rough slabs, formerly occupied by a large body of convicts, nominally employed in cultivation, but in reality doing next to nothing, and the results of their labours are, therefore not very perceptible. The barrack is an irregular quadrangle, enclosing a space of about half an acre, the walls of which appear to me not more than seven feet high, pierced with diminutive windows that afford little light and less ventilation, and you seem to feel their unwholesomeness the moment you enter them, and the less I say about the cleanliness of this neglected asylum the better. In fact, the edifice is as badly adapted for the purpose it is used for—a place of shelter for a people whom the viscissitudes of war have made us the natural guardians of—as could have been found.

In selecting a residence for them, it should have been remembered that they have not been nurtured like ourselves in houses, and the close unwholesome atmosphere of such low-roofed abodes must be peculiarly unsuited to a race of people, who, down to the time of their surrender, lived wholly abroad, breathing only the pure and uninfected air of their own glens.

This establishment is in a place so secluded, so completely away from all the chief thoroughfares of the island, and so rarely visited except by the inhabitants of the by-district it is placed in, chiefly sawyers and splitters, that I doubt if its very existence is known to the great bulk of the community; or that on the shores of an unfrequented bay are still to be found the remnants of those men who for so many years successfully held their ground against their powerful invaders, with a pertinacity that will long be remembered by the colonists; and if it is recorded of them that they committed many acts of aggression on the settlers, it will be at least admitted that it was not by their hands that the first blows were dealt, or the first blood drawn.* These circumstances, now that the strife is past, should make them the objects of our peculiar solicitude. Is there, then, nothing that we owe them beyond a naked sustenance and a deserted barrack? Should we be satisfied with voting them a few hundreds annually to prevent them dying of want? or at knowing they are at liberty to wander where they like in the bush, exposed to the demoralisation inseparable from constant contact with the restless community of bush sawyers, &c., whose acquaintance with the simple-minded women of the blacks is notoriously impure? or that we pay a non-resident superintendent to protect them, who might as well be in Spitzbergen as where he ever is, that is, absent from his post enjoying himself at head quarters? True, there are some inferior persons here, but whose care for the natives is confined, I believe, to the mere issue of such supplies as the Legislature allows the blacks and their dogs. But if it ever extends beyond this, all I can say is they are a greatly belied class.

It is a reproach to us that they are under no real supervision, and that nothing is done to raise them above their original condition, or rather that we have allowed them to sink still lower

---

* I had not read the Aboriginal Committee's Report when I wrote this.

than they were when we first found them. Let anyone who doubts this visit the district, and he will hear nothing to controvert it, or to show that either chastity in the women nor temperance in either sex are to be regarded as virtues, or that anything is done to arrest their degradation.

The natives are, at least nominally, Christians, and in the census of the colony are assigned to the Established Church, but it would be interesting to know when they last received instruction of any sort. In this they are wholly neglected. It is idle excusing ourselves from these duties, by saying that they are intractable and incapable of receiving instruction. On the contrary, I know they are naturally acute, cheerful, and no less intelligent than ourselves.

At the time of their surrender they numbered about 250, of whom about fifteen-sixteenths have died in only 20 years, a most fearful mortality. A few births added a trifle to their numbers. There now remain only 16 of pure-blood and one half-caste—a female. Of the former there are four men, two boys, and ten women. The boys are about 15 years of age, and must have been born since the surrender of the race. So there remain, of all that Robinson gathered together, only 14. There are now no births, though some of both sexes have not passed the prime of life.

What a melancholy state of things these facts disclose. But passing these over, it is impossible to help inquiring what causes could have led to the premature decadence of that portion of this people who survived the calamities of war, and what reason can can be assigned for their infertility since falling into our hands.

To the first of these questions I have often thought it might be replied, forcing on them too suddenly our own habits, as if the savage could at once adapt himself to the ways of civilised life; in fact, requiring a people whose whole lives had been passed in the open air, to dwell as we dwell, and live as we live. Into this error Robinson himself fell, for when he first drew the Bruny Islanders together around his dwelling, several died almost directly. * He housed, or rather huddled them together in warm rooms, and required them to wear clothing. But doubtless, this partial confinement in an atmosphere too impure for them, and the too sudden restraint of the free use of their limbs, were wholly unsuited to their habits and constitutions, and, of

---

* In the original I said six, which number I took from the grave mounds that I saw in 1830. I had not then read Robinson's report, giving the correct number of deaths, namely, 22, so that many bodies must have been disposed of in other ways than by burial.

course, when divested of these fatal comforts, colds, and the endless train of disorders that spring from them, sent them rapidly to the grave.

That so few births have happened since their captivity commenced (and even these appear now to have ceased) may perhaps be traced in some measure to the above causes, particularly to the entire change of habits. But if it is true, as I have repeatedly heard, that prostitution is commonly practised by the women, the chief cause of course lies here.

I have dwelt, perhaps, at too great length on the subject under review, but it is difficult to compress the account, of the condition of a people into a paragraph, and few, I hope, will begrudge the time expended on the perusal of this paper, who understand the duties of man to his fellows, and the consequent necessity of atoning for long neglect, even at this late hour, by future attention to their wants ; for we cannot by mere maintenance in life repay the debt we owe a race whom we have forcibly dispossessed of everything but mere existence. Other duties we are bound to take on ourselves, to improve the condition of the remnant whom time, war, and disease have left to our care, and by careful supervision to arrest the evils that are fast working out their extinction.

Appendix.

I HAVE said nothing of Colonel Arthur's project for capturing the aborigines--a scheme that was devised and attempted in 1830; and I shall here say as little as I can of this absurd passage in the history of the colony.

The ill advised operations that he then undertook against so clever and crafty a foe, that have received the designation of the "Black War," (whereby he thought to enclose them within a moving line, advancing from north to south on a point of the coast, where two large peninsulæ are united with the main by a narrow isthmus called East Bay Neck) was too chimerical in its conception, too absurd in its progress, and too inconsiderable in its results, to deserve serious notice. A line of troops and ready volunteers and others, numbering more than 4,000 * persons, was stretched across the midland and eastern districts, to advance in thin but regular array. These districts, though open and level in some parts, are, as a whole, woody and very hilly; and as unfavourable for military operations of any kind, unless perhaps defensive ones, as it is possible to imagine. No such line could possibly move in such a country, with any degree of regularity; nor could the necessary communications be kept up. Some of the many intervening eminences have more the aspect and general character of mountains than of ordinary hills, and here and there are so covered with underwood that a rat could hardly creep through; others are precipitous, and most of them very steep. The late Captain Vicary, of the 63rd, told me that in crossing a very rugged eminence, called the Blue-hill, between the Clyde and Shannon Rivers, with his company, each man marching as usual a few yards apart, the regularity of their advance was wholly broken in ten minutes, and to use his own expression, "The devil a man of them did he see the whole of the rest of the day;" and this was

---

* See Melville's "Van Diemen's Land Annual" (1833) page 94.

daily the case with many other parties. Such a line was of course no
line at all; and though for some weeks there were a tribe or two in its
front, directly the acute savage understood the nature of the game that
was going on, he burst through it and escaped, "leaving hardly a
wreck behind." Two men were, however, taken, and two others shot,
by a party led by a gentleman named Walpole (report, 29th October,
1830, Walpole's). This prize, such as it was, cost about £30,000. The
men belonged to the Big River and Oyster Bay tribes, who were then
united, as Robinson found them at the end of the next year. They
now consisted of 41 individuals, who, as we have preceedingly seen,
were reduced to 26 when caught. The plan of operations—conceived
in ignorance of the difficulty of its execution—necessarily ended
in failure.

Judged of by European standards of beauty, our natives were not
generally a good looking race. But then the custom of both sexes to
disfigure themselves—the men by smearing their heads with a compound
of grease and ochre, and the women by shaving the head, so as to
produce the appearance of absolute baldness—gave a repulsiveness of
look to them that was not natural Some of the youths of both sexes
were passable enough, and one woman, whom I remember, who
attracted crowds to see her when Robinson brought in the tribe she
belonged to, was remarkably handsome. Some of the men, too,
though very savage looking fellows, were, in most respects, in no way
the inferior of the European. A native of one of the West Coast tribes,
called Pen-ne-me-ric, whose portrait was painted with phothographic
exactness by an artizan of this town for transmission to Europe, possessed as fine and thoughtful features as anyone would desire to look
upon. No fair judgment of them is to be formed, either from the
paintings of Duttereau, or the few weird-looking old creatures that
photography has preserved from absolute forgetfulness, who seem to
have been selected from the most hideous of them

From the causes mentioned above, more than from any natural
defects, the most of them succeeded in making themselves repulsive
enough; but had it been passible to have placed them in more favourable circumstances than those in which we found them, I believe that
(colour apart) they would not have stood much behind any other race.

The following extract from a private letter of Robinson's to his
friend Mr. George Whitcomb, gives us his opinion of the apperarnce
and *physique* of the Tasmanian savage in his primitive state, or as he
seemed to him to be, immediately after his withdrawel from his native
wilds:—

"The undertaking in which I am engaged," that is against the
blacks, " has been crowned with complete success. The little colony
of blacks on Swan Island are all well and in excellent spirits. I fell in
with these near to George's River, and fifteen miles inland, and conducted them through the forest (a distance of forty-five miles) to Swan
Island. On this occasion I was only accompanied by one white man, as
servant, and was unarmed The aboriginies on Swan Island are a fine

race of people, and not that miserable race that some have represented (or rather misrepresented) the aboriginal of Van Diemen's Land to be. They are equal if not superior to many Europeans. The most fallacious reports have been circulated to the prejudice of these poor benighted creatures. I have not yet in my long walk round the island and through the interior, met with that degenerated race, that some have represented the aboriginal of Van Diemen's Land to be, &c., &c."

The walk he speaks of, is described in an early part of this volume, viz., the very circuitous one of a thousand miles, that he travelled on the occasion of visiting the tribes who dwelt in the country that lay between Spring River and Emu Bay.

ERRATUM,—At page 34 for *has been named before*, read, *will be named presently*.

HENN & Co., Printers, 12, & 75, Elizabeth-street, Hobart Town.

www.ingramcontent.com/pod-product-compliance
Lightning Source LLC
Chambersburg PA
CBHW020125170426
43199CB00009B/647